The New Deal & Modern American Conservatism

The New Deal & Modern American Conservatism

A Defining Rivalry

Gordon Lloyd and
David Davenport

HOOVER INSTITUTION PRESS
STANFORD UNIVERSITY   STANFORD, CALIFORNIA

The Hoover Institution on War, Revolution and Peace, founded at Stanford University in 1919 by Herbert Hoover, who went on to become the thirty-first president of the United States, is an interdisciplinary research center for advanced study on domestic and international affairs. The views expressed in its publications are entirely those of the authors and do not necessarily reflect the views of the staff, officers, or Board of Overseers of the Hoover Institution.

www.hoover.org

Hoover Institution Press Publication No. 642

Hoover Institution at Leland Stanford Junior University,
Stanford, California 94305-6010

First printing 2013
19 18 17 16 15 14 13   7 6 5 4 3 2 1

Manufactured in the United States of America

The paper used in this publication meets the minimum Requirements of
the American National Standard for Information Sciences—Permanence
of Paper for Printed Library Materials, ANSI/NISO Z39.48-1992. ♾

Cataloging-in-Publication Data is available from the Library of Congress.
ISBN: 978-0-8179-1684-8 (cloth. : alk. paper)
ISBN: 978-0-8179-1686-2 (e-book)

CONTENTS

PREFACE

In the aftermath of the 2012 presidential election, there is almost a frenzy to explain what went wrong with Republicans and what conservatives must do to be a viable part of the national conversation. "Whither conservatism?" seems to be the political question of the day. Our answer is: Go back to come back. History often contains signposts for the way forward, and we think that is most certainly the case here.

The particular historical trail we propose to travel in this book started when we taught a course to public policy graduate students on "The Roots of the American Order." We concluded that the American republic was defined and established in three crises during its history: (1) the Founding crisis, (2) the Civil War crisis, and (3) the Great Depression and New Deal crisis. We challenged students to understand what a crisis is, not from secondary sources but from the perspective of those who lived and led the way through it. Each of these crises defined or redefined the very nature of the American republic.

The more we studied the third crisis—the Great Depression and the New Deal of the 1930s—the more we realized it had established the frame for American domestic policy and the ongoing debate between progressives and conservatives today. The debates between Franklin Roosevelt and Herbert Hoover in the 1930s sound very much like the campaign rhetoric of liberals and conservatives in 2012. Roosevelt's New Deal established the infrastructure on which President Obama and the Democrats are still building and expanding government. And Herbert Hoover articulated the core principles of modern American conservatism that resonate today.

As two colleagues who have written twenty-five or so op-eds together in recent years, and who taught these ideas on the faculty of the School of Public Policy at Pepperdine University, we decided it might be valuable to write this book to illuminate this historic frame. Before collaborating on this book, Gordon Lloyd had edited a volume that used original speeches and documents to create the Hoover-Roosevelt debate that never really occurred face to face: *The Two Faces of Liberalism: How the Hoover-Roosevelt Debate Shapes the 21st Century* (M & M Scrivener Press, 2006). More recently, we made a fuller exploration of Herbert Hoover's record as a conservative, both before and during the New Deal, in coauthoring a chapter, "The Two Phases of Herbert Hoover's Constitutional Conservatism." This will appear in a book edited by Joseph Postell and Johnathan O'Neill, *Toward an American Conservatism: Constitutional Conservatism during the Progressive Era,* to be published by Palgrave McMillan in fall 2013.

In this book we go back again to the 1930s, but with the express purpose of coming back to public policy today. We seek to recapture a debate between Roosevelt and Hoover that has been lost, but which is timely today. In the name of addressing an economic emergency, an earlier generation was willing to trade in some of its liberty and reshape the republic on a temporary basis. But that emergency response never went away. Instead, it became what we call today "the new normal," a newly reshaped welfare state from which we continue to work, and to which we continue to add.

Chapter 1 reaches back to establish the New Deal frame and Herbert Hoover's response. Chapter 5 reaches forward to see where the debate might go from here, especially for conservatism. In the intervening chapters, 2 through 4, we take up what we see as the three pivotal issues, laying out the essence of the progressive-conservative debate between Hoover and Roosevelt in the 1930s in the first half of each chapter, then illustrating how those issues remain current in public policy today.

Our thanks to those who have assisted in our work on these Hoover-Roosevelt projects, including both the book chapter and this book: Tom Church and Carson Bruno, former Pepperdine students who are now at the Hoover Institution, and Dana O'Neill. And thanks also to Pepperdine graduate students Michael Crouch and Anthony Miller, who assisted in tracking down coverage of the fate of American conservatism.

CHAPTER 1

The New Deal and the Origin of Modern American Conservatism

THE NEW DEAL AND HOOVER'S BURKEAN MOMENT

It is widely claimed that modern American conservatism was born in the 1950s with the publication of William F. Buckley's *God and Man at Yale* in 1951, Russell Kirk's *The Conservative Mind* in 1953, and, perhaps most important, the founding of *National Review* in 1955.[1] The ideas advanced in these publications—limited government, moral truth, free markets, and American sovereignty and strength, as summarized in *National Review*'s founding mission— did launch an intellectual movement which soon enough advanced to the political arena, most visibly with the nomination of conservative Barry Goldwater for president in 1964 and the election of Ronald Reagan as president in 1980.

---

1. See for example, Jerome L. Himmelstein, *To the Right: The Transformation of American Conservatism* (Berkeley, CA: University of California Press, 1990), 15. See generally, George H. Nash, *The Conservative Intellectual Movement in America Since 1945* (Wilmington, DE: Intercollegiate Studies Institute, 1996), introduction and chapter 1.

But the search for the birth of modern American conservatism needs to reach back further than the 1950s. Even as the French Revolution of the eighteenth century prompted Edmund Burke's foundational conservative document, *Reflections on the Revolution in France,* establishing Burke as the father of modern conservatism, so too did modern America have its own revolution, President Franklin Roosevelt's New Deal, and its own contemporary conservative respondent, Herbert Hoover. Indeed, Hoover's and Roosevelt's writings and speeches, beginning with their presidential campaign in 1932, but especially after the New Deal began to be implemented in 1933, frame the progressive-conservative debate that has dominated the American political and policy landscape for the last eighty years and is still going strong.

In retrospect, we can now see more clearly that the New Deal was America's French Revolution, and the post-presidential Herbert Hoover, if not our Edmund Burke, was at least a prophetic voice crying in the progressive wilderness of the 1930s, pointing the way toward what has become modern American conservatism. As the influential conservative Frank Meyer wrote, the conservative *movement* of the 1950s was a delayed reaction to the New Deal.[2] But it's useful to return to both the New Deal revolution itself and the real-time reaction provided by Herbert Hoover.

When Hoover saw the revolutionary nature of the New Deal unfolding, he had what we might call a Burkean moment: a realization that to be an American conservative meant no longer cooperating or temporizing with progressivism within the American System, but shifting to become a defender of the American System against a progressive assault. In his public leadership as secretary of commerce and then as president, Hoover felt that progressivism could be assimilated into the American System through his two-fold

---

2. Frank S. Meyer, "Conservatism," in *Left, Right, and Center: Essays on Liberalism and Conservatism in the United States,* ed. Robert Goldwin (Chicago: Rand McNally, 1965), 1–17, at 3.

approach of "American individualism" and "constructive govern-ment." But in this later phase, dominated by the sweeping changes of the New Deal, Hoover became a full-throated constitutional con-servative, horrified by what he called the challenge to liberty from Roosevelt's New Deal.[3] He saw the very constitutional system itself, as well as the constitutional morality of the American people, poi-soned by "a revolutionary design to replace the American System with despotism."[4]

What exactly did Hoover mean by the American System? He meant a system in which individual freedom and equal opportu-nity lead to a sense of responsibility which inspires Americans to take care of each other while pursuing their own and their com-munities' best interests, unhindered by government bureaucracy or central planning, both of which lead to despotism. The American System limits government to those areas where it can do the most good (public education, the Federal Reserve System, maintenance of protective tariffs) but otherwise trusts public life to the self-government of individuals acting in voluntary cooperation, from labor relations and scientific research to religious expression and charitable organizations.

Even as historian J.G.A. Pocock argued that revolutionaries con-front a "Machiavellian Moment" when they come face to face with the problem of how to govern,[5] a Burkean moment occurs when conservatives come face to face with the problem of how to resist revolutionary change with which they strongly disagree. There are

---

3. Joseph Postell and Johnathan O'Neill, eds., *Toward an American Conservatism: Constitutional Conservatism during the Progressive Era* (New York: Palgrave Macmillan, publication expected 2013).

4. See Gordon Lloyd, ed., *The Two Faces of Liberalism: How the Hoover-Roosevelt Debate Shapes the 21st Century* (Salem, MA: M & M Scrivener Press, 2007), 123–139, where Hoover contrasts the American System of ordered liberty with a new deal that would "alter the whole foundations of our national life."

5. J.G.A. Pocock, *The Machiavellian Moment: Florentine Political Thought and the Atlantic Republican Tradition* (Princeton, NJ: Princeton University Press, 1975).

really two choices: to flee or to fight. When Hoover understood, like Burke in his day, that a revolution in values and institutions was taking place, he sought to stop it in its tracks. In fact, the record shows that the one person who spoke most, wrote most, and campaigned most—and most coherently—against the New Deal as it unfolded was Herbert Hoover. And even though he was unable to persuade a majority of Americans at the time, his arguments against the New Deal's transformation of America laid out the case that would eventually become known as modern American conservatism.[6]

TWO REVOLUTIONARY MOMENTS

Richard Price, the British moral philosopher and preacher of the eighteenth century, argued that there was a fundamental harmony among the Glorious English Revolution of 1688, the American Revolution of 1776, and the French Revolution of 1789. All three revolutions, Price argued, represented the almost inevitable victory of the forces of democracy over the old and unjust monarchical and aristocratic order. Not so, said his countryman Edmund Burke, pointing out that the French Revolution was different in character from its English and American counterparts. The French Revolution was dangerous, Burke wrote, because it was driven by "envy," especially envy toward the holders of property. It contemplated nothing less than the total destruction of the old order, since the revolutionaries despised the past, and a complete revamping of the role that government would play in the daily life of the people. It was as though Burke understood that the British and American revolutions were fundamentally political, whereas the French Revolution was primarily social in nature.[7]

6. Herbert Hoover, *The Challenge to Liberty* (New York: Charles Scribner's Sons, 1934), and his 1928 campaign speeches in *Two Faces of Liberalism*, 35–47.

7. Edmund Burke, *Reflections on the Revolution in France* (Indianapolis: Liberty Fund, 1999). He wrote this as a response to Richard Price's 1789 sermon, *A Discourse*

It is useful to distinguish a political revolution—a fundamental alteration in the form of government—such as occurred in Britain and the United States from the larger social revolution in France. The British revolution constitutionalized the monarchy. The American Revolution replaced the British monarchy and its overseas empire with thirteen state-based republics joined together in a federal union. The Founders debated for eighty-eight days how to construct the legislative, executive, and judicial branches, as well as how to divide the powers between the nation and the states. But not once did they debate social issues such as public relief, national festivals, or *ancien* regimes. Burke said the American and British revolutions were essentially restorations, but the French Revolution was a dangerous and total transformation of the political, social, and economic order into something the world had never before seen. This was a true revolution, one that was linear and thus progressive, not circular and restorative in character.

The case for the French Revolution is found in the works of J.J. Rousseau and his protégés. Their approach focuses not on governmental structures but on community, solidarity, and ensuring égalité (what we would call today equality of outcome). Competition is opposed because of its supposed vices of selfishness and greed. At the core of the Rousseau narrative is a turning away from the very existence of wealth and its unequal distribution which comes with the improvement of the human condition. Instead, he held that a system that abides or even encourages competition is socially and ethically flawed because it produces an unacceptable distribution of property and power. This, of course, has become the philosophy behind the equality narrative that was part and parcel of the New Deal as well as public policy in the age of President Obama. The social issue becomes a political issue and the role of government

---

on the Love of our Country, republished in *The Norton Anthology of English Literature, 8th edition* (New York: W.W. Norton & Company, 2006).

shifts from being an arbiter of the disputes among the numerous and varied interests of society to being a major player in the production and distribution of national income and wealth.[8]

The Burkean moment then, experienced by Hoover in the 1930s and by conservatives ever since, was the realization that liberty is in danger. It is not so much that Western civilization is in danger as that American liberty is in danger. As Hoover said of Roosevelt then, and many have said of Obama today, the progressive regime would move America more toward the European model of statism and socialism-lite. It would turn its back on constitutional government established by the Founders to the extent necessary to achieve its social and political goals. Hoover's Burkean moment prompted him to realize that the very nature of the American regime was changing with the New Deal and that these fundamental and sweeping changes had to be resisted. Thus was modern American conservatism born as a response to the revolutionary New Deal.

THE NEW DEAL AND HOOVER'S RESPONSE

Franklin Roosevelt saw the 1932 election as an opportunity to transform the American System from its attachment to a conservative past to a utopian quest for a secure future. The federal government should "assume bold leadership," he said in his July 2, 1932, address accepting the presidential nomination, noting that the laws of economics to which Herbert Hoover and others had been attached were not "sacred, inviolable, unchangeable" at all, but made by human beings. As political scientist and historian Ira Katznelson

8. J.J. Rousseau, *The First and Second Discourses*, ed. Roger D. Masters (New York: St. Martin's Press, 1964); Rousseau, *On the Social Contract*, ed. Roger D. Masters, (New York, St. Martin's Press, 1978). For our purposes, it is sufficient to note that Rousseau and his followers argued that private property is theft and that individual rights generally are derived from and are subject to the will of the community. Furthermore, political institutions such as the separation of powers and federalism are undemocratic restraints on the direct and authentic voice of the people.

concluded in his recent book: "In a decisive break with the old, the New Deal intentionally crafted not just a new set of policies but also new forms of institutional meaning, language, and possibility for a model that had been invented 150 years before," adding that it "retrofit[ted] capitalism and shap[ed] a welfare state."[9]

In the breathless first hundred days of the New Deal, a vast array of emergency legislation was enacted. Although these enactments were considered by Congress, they were drafted by the executive branch and subjected to very little debate. Part of the New Deal revolution that has persisted is that these new measures consistently shifted power from the legislature to the expert administrators of the executive branch. In all, some forty new administrative agencies, referred to by historians as the alphabet soup agencies, were formed in the first year of the New Deal. The most sweeping law, the National Industrial Recovery Act, gave the president incredibly broad new powers over industry and enabled the creation of massive public works programs. Republican Congressman Charles Eaton of New Jersey said at the time that it was the New Deal's effort "to remake the entire structure" of American capitalism. The US Supreme Court later ruled that its broad delegation of power to the executive branch was unconstitutional, though much of the law remained.[10] As is noted in chapter 3, the federal government grew dramatically in size and power during the New Deal.

In the name of taming an economic crisis, President Roosevelt undertook emergency measures to reshape the federal government, few of which went away when the recovery was completed. Roosevelt practiced what President Obama's former chief of staff, Rahm Emanuel, later preached: it's a shame to waste a good crisis. In a very real sense, the New Deal managed to reinvent and reshape

9. Ira Katznelson, *Fear Itself: The New Deal and the Origins of Our Time* (New York: Liveright Publ. Corp., 2012), 6 ff.

10. A.L.A. Schechter Poultry Corp. v. United States, 295, US 495, 55 S. Ct. 837, 79 L. Ed. 1570 (1935).

the federal government in ways that still form the basic shape of American domestic policy today.

Even before the New Deal was implemented, Herbert Hoover saw that Roosevelt intended major changes. In a speech at Madison Square Garden on October 31, 1932, near the end of the presidential campaign, Hoover said that Roosevelt's proposed programs were not the kind of "change that comes from normal development of national life," rather proposing to "alter the whole foundation of our national life . . . and of the principles upon which we have builded the nation." In particular, Hoover continued, over against the decentralization and self-government intended by the Founders, Roosevelt proposed a "centralization of government [that] will undermine responsibilities and destroy the system." The New Deal proposals, he concluded, "represent a radical departure from the foundations of 150 years which have made this the greatest nation in the world." In a statement that affirms the argument of this book, Hoover said the 1932 election was "a contest between two philosophies of government" and would decide "the direction our nation will take over a century to come."

We find in Hoover's response to Roosevelt's New Deal two fundamental arguments that frame the philosophy of modern American conservatism. First, Hoover argued that the New Deal challenged individual liberty, which was not only a political but also a moral and even spiritual matter. Second, it also challenged the Constitution, both the fundamental rights it guarantees and its system of a decentralized government of checks and balances and balances of power. Instead, the New Deal would transform the federal government's role into one of heavy regulation and regimentation. These core conservative messages, which constitute the origin of twentieth-century American conservatism, are—or at least should be—the core message of conservatives even today.[11]

---

11. We rely heavily on the original Roosevelt and Hoover source material selected and edited by Gordon Lloyd. See Lloyd, ed., *The Two Faces of Liberalism.*

THE CHALLENGE TO LIBERTY

Hoover's first tenet was that the New Deal challenged individual liberty, a message that resonated more powerfully then than today when people, especially younger people, have become more comfortable with big government. In his 1934 book, *The Challenge to Liberty,* he argued that "the spiritual and intellectual freedoms cannot thrive except when there are also economic freedoms." This argument was central to the later contributions of F.A. von Hayek in *The Road to Serfdom* and Milton Friedman's *Capitalism and Freedom,* two books that have guided twenty-first-century defenders of conservatism. In his "Crisis to Free Men" speech on June 10, 1936, at the Republican National Convention, Hoover argued that the Roosevelt programs had crushed "the first safeguard of liberty" in their quest for a new order by the substitution of personal power for independently cast electoral votes. In his 1938 speech, "The Challenge to Liberty," Hoover again argued that philosophical case for liberty, pointing out that there had been "a gigantic shift of government from the function of umpire to the function of directing, dictating, and competing in our economic life."

But there was an important new emphasis in Hoover's defense of liberty that was not as prominent in the pre–New Deal Hoover, namely that "liberty is an endowment from the Creator of every individual man and woman upon which no power . . . may deny." This appeal to "unalienable rights" as the moral foundation of liberty was not in the forefront of Hoover's earlier work, when he thought that the American contribution to "human betterment" was based in the blending of traditional American values of rugged individualism and equality of opportunity with the "constructive government" contribution of a tamed progressivism.[12]

---

12. Herbert Hoover, *Challenge to Liberty,* 3.

Armed with this foundational change of emphasis, Hoover revisited the values articulated in his 1922 *American Individualism* pamphlet and his 1928 campaign speeches. He wanted to make sure that the reader recognized that there was a two-fold continuity in his overall defense of the American System since the 1920s: It is "no system of laissez faire" and liberty and progress go together.[13] In the language of his earlier work, there was a fundamental compatibility between American individualism and constructive government. The notion that government should do next to nothing and business should do as it pleases, and that "every man for himself" should prevail, "has been dead in America for generations," Hoover said.[14] It was trotted out in these heady days of the New Deal, Hoover added, as "political invective for a long list of collectivist writers who infer that it dominated and directed the policies of the United States up to some recent date, when it was suddenly vanquished—and abandoned." Hoover described this interpretation as no more than dishonest polemic and pointed out what he said in his 1922 *American Individualism*: we abandoned laissez faire "when we adopted the ideal of equality of opportunity—the fair chance of Abraham Lincoln."[15]

Interestingly Hayek also said in *The Road to Serfdom* that he was not defending laissez faire, which he saw as a term hauled out by critics of free markets as an easy way to promote socialism in the 1940s. By the early twentieth century the term laissez faire had

13. Lloyd, *The Two Faces of Liberalism,* 38.

14. Herbert Hoover, *The Challenge to Liberty,* 51.

15. Herbert Hoover, *American Individualism* (New York: Doubleday-Page Publishers, 1922). Hoover sees Lincoln as not only the moral founder of the Republican Party, but also the person who best understood what it means to be an American. Although Hoover does not rely on any explicit Lincoln textual references, we suggest that Hoover holds Lincoln's Emancipation Proclamation and Gettysburg Address in high regard. The first is a defense of individual liberty against slavery and the second asks whether the experiment in representative government shall endure.

acquired the negative meaning of leaving things as they are or let-ting the government do nothing. The earlier nineteenth-century meaning of laissez faire was that we should let individuals make their own decisions concerning their daily lives. The government should become involved in a necessary few and carefully defined areas such as common defense and public tranquility and in poli-cies that advanced the infrastructure of a market economy. These should certainly be core values of modern American conservatism today.

So part of the challenge to liberty was defining what liberty is and is not. While Hoover was clearing away the laissez faire under-brush, he turned to the term "rugged individualism," which he had used during the 1920s to describe the nature of the American System. By rugged individualism, Hoover emphasized, he did not mean a "heartless disregard for the 'public welfare.'" Rather, he used it in both the 1920s and the 1930s as Americans had used it for over half a century: "in eulogy of those God-fearing men and women of honesty whose stamina and character and fearless assertion of rights led them to make their own way in life." But by the 1930s, rugged individualism, just like laissez faire, had acquired the nega-tive connotation of personal selfishness and a total disregard for the well-being, or even the plight, of the unfortunate—or, as Roosevelt liked to personify them, the "forgotten man."

THE REVOLUTIONARY NEW DEAL

According to Hoover, the roots of the American order were *forgot-ten* on March 3, 1933. We may accept that the date of creation was moved to March 4, the day on which Roosevelt took the oath of office. We think that Hoover had the revolutionary nature of the New Deal dead right. As for Roosevelt, in his "Long Range Planning" speech (October 31, 1932), his fireside chat on the New Deal (May 7, 1933), and his State of the Union address (January 3, 1936), he articulated a self-understanding that a new American order began with his inauguration on March 4, 1933. It was an order whose work of transformation of American values from individualism to communitarianism is still in progress.

Interestingly, for the development of modern American conservatism, the most important chapter in Hayek's *Road to Serfdom* is called "The Abandoned Road." Hayek located the origin of the European abandonment of the classical liberal road in an intellectual crisis in late nineteenth-century Germany. The intellectuals, he argued, turned their backs on the tradition of Western civilization. A mere fifty years later, all Europe was operating within this statist model. Would America be next? In his *Memoirs on the Great Depression, 1929–1941,* Hoover suggested that Roosevelt had surrounded himself with intellectuals who wished to transform America into Europe. "All these various forms of collectivist philosophy merely differ in degree and kinds of servitudes," Hoover said; they are all part of the regimentation of men and are all opposed to "True American Liberalism." Hoover's critique of "collectivist philosophy" could not have been said better by Hayek a decade later in *The Road to Serfdom* or by Hannah Arendt in her 1948 book *On Totalitarianism,* in which she upset the Left by saying that fascism, Nazism, and communism were each species of totalitarianism.[16]

As early as 1934, Hoover appealed to the Declaration of Independence and the Bill of Rights as expressions of "a new liberty of men" in addition to the Civil War amendments and the Nineteenth Amendment securing the right to vote for women. So, yes, while there was still an appeal to the evolutionary character of the American heritage of the never wholly realized ideals of liberty

---

16. See F.A. Hayek, *The Road to Serfdom: Text and Documents, The Definitive Edition,* ed. Bruce Caldwell (Chicago: University of Chicago Press, 2007). Hayek claims that, in effect, there was a fork in the road and, sometime in late nineteenth-century Germany, intellectuals abandoned the road of liberty in favor of the road to serfdom.

and progress, now there was a warmer and stronger appeal beyond Lincoln and the progressives to the Founding itself. We now learn that "until recently, in all of our continuous adjustments we have preserved the great individual rights with which men were endowed by the Creator. . . . The most gigantic step," said Hoover, "that a nation can take is to shift its fundamental philosophic and social ideas."[17]

Also critical to his defense of liberty, then, was how to answer the following question: "Is the Great Depression the product of the economic system of Liberty? Can this system furnish recovery from it?" "No," was his answer to the first question, since "this depression is the direct result of government actions" at home and abroad and not the result of something inherent in the American economic order. "Yes," was Hoover's composite answer to the second question, noting that we were on our way to recovery from the Depression by the summer of 1932. Thus the election of 1932, "with its determination of an abrupt change in national policies," interrupted "the march of confidence and recovery." "Recovery from this depression is inevitable," Hoover said, "though it may be slowed up by governmental policies." We should follow this path of natural liberty for which our fathers died, he added.

Hoover's main point throughout was that "in America, where Liberty blazed brightest and by its glow shed light to all others, it is today impaired and endangered."[18] And that was because the New Deal had replaced the transitory and evolutionary nature of the American System with a project that "steps off the solid highways of true American Liberty into the dangerous quicksands of governmental direction."

17. Herbert Hoover, *The Memoirs of Herbert Hoover: The Great Depression, 1929–1941* (New York: The MacMillan Company, 1952), 381. What Hayek calls the road to serfdom, Hoover calls the bureaucratic "pavement of the collectivist highway."

18. Herbert Hoover, *The Challenge to Liberty,* 190–193.

THE NEW DEAL AND MODERN AMERICAN CONSERVATISM

So what exactly was the New Deal doing that was so different and dangerous to American values? And, how does Hoover's reaction contain the roots of modern American conservatism? Hoover would outline the responses as follows: 1) We unloaded on our children unnecessary debt and a regimented life rather than the blessings of liberty. 2) We deviated from the Founders and their notion of unalienable rights and from the doctrine of the Declaration and the unalienable liberties and personal securities which it implies. 3) These blessings are currently denounced by intellectuals in stark contrast to the American people, for whom the principles of liberty and security are embedded in their daily thought and action. 4) These blessings are embedded in the institutional structure of the Constitution. This fundamental document was not devised simply with regard to interstate commerce or the determination of weights and measures and coinage. No, as Hoover said, the Constitution was designed to guarantee fundamental liberties apart from the state.[19]

Meanwhile, Hoover stood firm in his defense of constitutional government, calling for a reinvigorated attachment to the separation of powers in the federal government; the line of demarcation between the federal and state governments; the Bill of Rights; and the electoral system itself, all of which were part of the Founders' design. Unfortunately, Hoover noted, the New Deal violated constitutional federalism by its "vast centralization of power in the Executive." Such centralization of power in the hands of bureaucrats armed with utopian ideas of national planning, to be implemented by coercive execution and coercive cooperation, undermined the separation of powers. Hoover pointed specifically to the practices of regimenting industry and commerce to eliminate unfair competitive practices, regimenting agriculture by telling farmers when to sow and reap, competing with business as in the Tennessee Valley

19. Ibid., 194–206.

Authority, managing currency and credit, and so forth. All this, Hoover said, amounted to "a vast shift from the American concept of human rights" and a "vast casualty to Liberty if it shall be continued."[20]

The false liberalism of the New Deal was governmental dictation and operation of commerce, industry, and agriculture, according to Hoover. In 1935, he urged the abolition of the National Recovery Act: it was the equivalent of fascist regimentation and an abandonment of "the principles of real social justice upon which this Nation was founded." The act violated the spirit and letter of the Constitution. "True Liberalism," which was the cornerstone of Hoover's constitutional conservatism, sees securing the blessings of liberty in the Constitution as the top priority of the exceptional American System.

In his *Memoirs,* Hoover identified the Election of 1932 as "a turning point in American life—and possibly the world." It attempted to transform America and revolutionize the world. The whole purpose of the New Deal was to make America over, and this involved an alteration in American values and a collectivist reading of the Constitution. This is what we have called a Burkean moment.

CONCLUSION

According to Hoover, the Great Depression offered three choices of action for the federal government:

- Do nothing, or "leave-it-alone liquidation."

- Do something to restore confidence through cooperation while adhering "rigidly to the Constitution and the liberties of the people."

20. Ibid., 103.

- Do everything, which would create a state-controlled economic system.

Hoover chose the second option. One gets the feeling that is what he thought Lincoln would do. But the Democrats accused him, as do many historians, of following the first option. They insisted that Hoover was personally responsible for the Great Depression and that he did nothing about it. Hoover felt Roosevelt was headed toward the third option.

But Hoover was an optimistic constitutional conservative. And so, on October 24, 1940, on the eve of Roosevelt's attempt to secure the presidency for an unprecedented third term, he delivered a radio address. "I do not suggest that Mr. Roosevelt aspires to be a dictator," he began. Nevertheless, he built "personal power to a dangerous point in the Republic." In his *Memoirs,* Hoover noted that Roosevelt showed his dictatorial taste by reducing both Congress and the judiciary to a rubber stamp and then issuing 1,486 executive orders in his first term in office. This was nearly equal to all the executive orders issued previously. A constitutional amendment securing presidential term limits, along with the resurgence of an independent Congress and Supreme Court as well as a rebirth of decentralized federalism, should count as victories for Hoover's constitutional conservatism in the 1930s.

It was the post-presidential Herbert Hoover who, alarmed by the excesses of the New Deal, pointed to the ideas that would constitute modern American conservatism. Whereas the proponents of the New Deal believed it was government's role to pursue equality of outcome for every man, Hoover pointed away from such a European model back toward the distinctive American ideals of liberty, equality of opportunity, and the fair chance of Abraham Lincoln. When Roosevelt grew the size and reach of the federal government dramatically, it was Hoover who pointed out the debilitating effect of government regimentation on free markets and a free society and made the case for limited government. When the New Deal would readily overlook the protections of the Constitution whenever "we the people" wanted to, it was Hoover who reargued the Founders' case for federalism and the right of the people to be protected from their government. These three pillars—liberty, limited government, and constitutionalism—formed the core of Herbert Hoover's case against the New Deal, and in turn became the underlying philosophy of modern American conservatism today.

CHAPTER 2

Liberty versus Equality

When an incumbent president runs for reelection, as Herbert Hoover did in 1932, the election is generally a referendum on his first term in office. At the same time, presidential campaigns present voters with contrasting visions of the road ahead. These descriptions certainly fit the 1932 campaign, with Hoover defending his constructive government-American individualism approach to the presidency and Franklin Roosevelt calling for a greatly expanded role for the federal government. Their clashing visions—liberty versus equality and equality of opportunity versus equality of outcome—provide a useful introduction to the issues at the heart of both the 1932 and the 2012 campaigns. They also illustrate one of the enduring conflicts between progressives and conservatives.

As the 1932 campaign unfolded, the debate pitted Hoover's constructive government and American individualism against Roosevelt's proposed communitarianism, or collective action, which Hoover later described as regimented government. By the end of the campaign it was, as Hoover observed in a campaign speech on October 31, 1932, "a contest between two philosophies of government," one a system of ordered liberty grounded in equality of opportunity, the other a promise of "new deals which would destroy the very foundations of our American System."

ROOSEVELT'S EGALITARIAN AGENDA

In a commencement address on May 22, 1932, Franklin Roosevelt pressed the theme that, in the wake of the Great Depression, happy times would not return without "the building of plans." Due to the absence of planning, he said, the graduating students were worse off than when they entered the university. Four years ago, they had entered with the expectation of a job awaiting them upon graduation, but there were no guaranteed jobs to be had. The Oglethorpe University graduates were characterized as victims of the established economic order. The failure of the market, they were told, must give way to the egalitarianism of the government.

In themes that resonated with the 2012 presidential campaign, Roosevelt identified the unequal distribution of national income generated by the market as the cause of the failure of the graduates to be guaranteed jobs. But, he said, with bold, persistent experimentation and planning, "we can bring about a wiser, more equitable distribution of national income." The connection among market failure, economic reform, economic recovery, national planning, emergency mobilization, the forgotten victim, and the happy times that would soon be here were vital to the New Deal project.

In his presidential nomination acceptance address, delivered on July 2, 1932, Roosevelt called for a New Deal: "I pledge you, I pledge myself, to a new deal for the American people. Let us all here assembled constitute ourselves prophets of a new order of competence and of courage. This is more than a political campaign, this is a call to arms." In a preview of later trickle-down economics, Roosevelt called for a crusade to rid America of the reactionary economics of "Toryism," the doctrine that, he said, falsely claimed that by increasing the prosperity of the few, wealth "will leak through" to everyone at the lowest level. The crusading imagery reached its climax in his March 4, 1933, inaugural address: ". . . we must move as a trained and loyal army willing to sacrifice for the good of a common discipline, because without such discipline no progress is made, no leadership becomes effective."

Roosevelt's remarkable September 23, 1932, Commonwealth Club Speech declared that the Jeffersonian idea of democracy—Hoover's rugged individualism plus constructive government—should be consigned to the dustbin of history. Instead, America should acknowledge the basic division of interests between capital and labor. Consequently, the fate of "everyman," rather than individual man, should be our guide. America should adopt the equality rather than the liberty narrative. "Clearly," Roosevelt proclaimed, "all this calls for a re-appraisal of values." In particular, America should recognize that the era of the "mere builder of more industrial plants . . . is as likely to be a danger as a help. The day of the great promoter or the financial Titan . . . is over." All this added up to nothing less than a new understanding of the role of government, and thus the nature of American values and of constitutional government itself. As Roosevelt said: "The day of enlightened administration" has come.

Advancing ideas that were still being debated in the campaign of 2012, Roosevelt proposed a new political economy, one that would shift the emphasis from the production to the distribution of wealth. This transformation required economic organizations to be responsible to the people rather than entrepreneurs acting each for himself. What we needed, according to Roosevelt, was an "economic declaration of rights, an economic constitutional order." And along with this new constitutional and egalitarian order—one which called for the demise of the separation of powers and decentralized federalism and the rise of the centralized administrative state—also came a new understanding of the Constitution and the

Declaration of Independence, where everyone has a constitutional right and governmental guarantee to freedom from fear and want.

HOOVER'S LIBERTY AGENDA

Hoover's June 10, 1936, "Crisis to Free Men" speech, which he prepared for the Republican National Convention, laid out the issue between liberty and equality very clearly: the New Deal had crushed "the first safeguard of liberty" in its quest for a new order by the substitution of personal power and the spoils system for independently cast electoral votes. Echoing the Founding generation's call for a government based on deliberation and choice, Hoover claimed that the 1932 election had actually emulated the "weapons of promise and hate" used by European socialist and fascist dictatorships. And this was the first step to "regimenting the people into a planned economy."

Hoover's April 8, 1938, speech in San Francisco, titled "The Challenge to Liberty," catalogued the change from liberty to equality: there had been "a gigantic shift of government from the function of umpire to the function of directing, dictating, and competing in our economic life." He applied "one test to the whole gamut of government action:" Does the action "stifle initiative and enterprise? Does it cost men their jobs?" Hoover's conclusion was quite practical: when the New Deal began in 1933, there were 12 million people unemployed and, in 1938, there were still 12 million people unemployed. In exchange, America had lost its liberty and become a regimented nation.

TWO ICONS OF THE 1930S MEET

What happens, then, when Hoover's rugged individual meets Roosevelt's forgotten man? According to Roosevelt, in his January 20, 1937, second inaugural address, it meant that one-third of the nation became "ill-housed, ill-clad, and ill-nourished." The American System, as it currently existed, was rigged to thwart the goals of democracy, which Roosevelt saw as an unending quest on behalf of "everyman." Accordingly, we needed to "change the moral climate of America" from a concern for the individual man to a concern for the forgotten man, or everyman. By 1937, Roosevelt claimed that, as a result of the New Deal programs, "I am justified in believing that the greatest change we have witnessed has been the change in the moral climate of America." The "test of our progress," Roosevelt emphasized "is not whether we add more to the abundance of those who have much; it is whether we provide enough for those who have too little." Thus the federal government—the "people's government"—guided by enlightened administrators, rather than the market controlled by the speculative entrepreneur, would become the provider of the necessities and conveniences of life for everyman. Heedless self-interest had been replaced by "the new order of . . . social justice."[1]

A composite of Hoover's response to this challenge was that the more accurate estimate of the less fortunate in America was closer to 25 percent than to one-third. And there was the distinction between the truly needy and the not-so-truly needy in that 25 percent. Moreover, he reminded his audience, we should not forget the 75 percent who are more, not less, fortunate; they are testimony to the success of the American System and its emphasis on individual liberty. "Through them is the sole hope for the 25 percent. If they be harassed, coerced, intimidated, discouraged, unduly taxed, the whole fabric will fall," Hoover said. The New Deal introduced the possibility of replacing the rugged individual with the

---

1. See Lloyd, ed., *The Two Faces of Liberalism*, for a collection of original addresses and speeches by both Roosevelt and Hoover. See pages 307–312 for Roosevelt's second inaugural address. See also Herbert Hoover, *Addresses Upon the American Road, 1933–1938* (New York: Charles Scribner's Sons, 1938), especially 53–56 and 216–220.

dependent individual. In so doing, the New Deal turned its back on the heritage of American liberty, tempered by a concern for those in distress. As mentioned in the previous chapter, Hoover considered the New Deal to have introduced a new calendar "that marks the creation of a new order of the ages."[2]

Hoover was concerned that there were people in America claiming "that Liberty has failed; that emergency encroachments upon its principles should be made permanent." In fact, he said, ". . . liberalism is now under beleaguered attack even in the great countries of its origins." A mere twenty years ago, he stated, we fought to make the world safe for democracy. Today, ". . . men freely debate how much of these (liberties) we will surrender." The European experience showed that "the dreams of those who saw Utopia are shattered and the people find they are marching backward toward the Middle Ages—as regimented men."[3]

HOOVER: AMERICA DOES NOT NEED SYSTEMIC CHANGE

Nevertheless, Hoover was optimistic, claiming that America was exceptional and the best hope for mankind. "The hope of America and the world is to regenerate Liberty with its responsibilities and its obligations—not to abandon it," he said. This regeneration of liberty with responsibility required a stronger foundational creed on which to rest the rejuvenation than his appeal to human evolution or a "developing creed" in America that he articulated in the 1920s. In his earlier work, *American Individualism*, Hoover referred

2. See especially Herbert Hoover, *Addresses Upon the American Road*, 56–93, for Hoover's explicit coverage of the 75 percent doing well under the American System over against the arrival of "the dependent individual." See also Hoover, *The Challenge to Liberty*, 95, for Hoover's remark about the new date of creation. This composite is drawn from a variety of addresses and speeches collected and edited by Lloyd, *The Two Faces of Liberalism*.

3. See especially Hoover, *The Challenge to Liberty*, 12–35.

to the developing creed of the American System expressed in contrast to the fixed, utopian, and failed nature of other philosophies. "They all have in common the idea of the servitude of the individual to the state, and the denial of liberties unassailable by the state," Hoover wrote. "All these various forms of collectivist philosophy merely differ in degree and kinds of servitudes." They are all part of the regimentation of men and are all opposed to "True American Liberalism."[4]

Hoover admitted that there had been abuses to liberty by, among others, greedy speculators. But he argued that these marginal abuses were no reason to substitute regimentation for liberty. These "marginal problems" can be cured by "the dynamic forces of Liberty." "We dwell greatly upon the abuses and weaknesses of our system, exaggerating them out of all proportion," he added. Accordingly, "the opponents of the American System cite these misuses of Liberty as if they were its overwhelming characteristics." But the right to liberty comes with the obligation to use liberty responsibly: "It is a denial of the right to use it for (economic) oppression."[5]

So what exactly was the New Deal doing that was different and dangerous to American values? We unloaded on our children unnecessary debt and a regimented life rather than the blessings of liberty, Hoover said. We deviated from the Founders and their notion of unalienable rights as well as the doctrine of the Declaration and the "unalienable liberties and personal securities," he continued. These blessings "are currently denounced" by the intellectuals with

4. Herbert Hoover, *American Individualism* (New York: Doubleday-Page Publishers, 1922), 4–5. Hoover contrasts five "old world" collectivist philosophies of government with the New World approach of American individualism based in "equality of opportunity—the fair chance of Abraham Lincoln." See also Hoover, *The Challenge to Liberty*.

5. Hoover, *The Challenge to Liberty*, 157. Also see Lloyd, *The Two Faces of Liberalism*, 390.

their dishonesty in stark contrast to the American people for whom the "principles of liberty and security are embedded in their daily thought and action."[6] These blessings were embedded in the institutional structure of the Constitution.[7]

The first two years of Franklin Roosevelt's New Deal prompted Hoover to see that the threats of totalitarianism were no longer thousands of miles across the ocean in Europe, as he had observed in his 1922 *American Individualism* essay, but were now visible at home in America. Hoover would say in a later speech, in March 1938: "If our own so-called planned economy is not an infection from the original stream of fascism it is at least a remarkable coincidence." Hoover feared that Americans were about to follow Europeans in trading their individual liberties for both individual and communal security.

ECONOMIC REGIMENTATION AND LIBERTY

In short, Hoover felt that economic regimentation by the government was rapidly eroding American liberty, a process which he traced step by step. "The first step of economic Regimentation is a vast centralization of power in the Executive," he said, putting American liberty to the test with powerful bureaucrats armed with utopian ideas of national planning. These bureaucrats had become "masters . . . of our daily lives," Hoover said, without the actual knowledge needed to run the daily lives of 125 million people, since the "bureaucracy cannot replace the judgment of millions of individuals striving in their own interests." In turn, the bureaucratic planners were frustrated by their inability to control or, in Hoover's words, "know the destiny of economic forces." It was a vicious cycle, with planners unable to control economic

6. Hoover had such intellectuals as Rexford Tugwell, Harold Ickes, and Henry Wallace in mind.

7. See especially Hoover, *The Challenge to Liberty*, 194–202.

forces, yet seeking more power to control the very forces they could not control.[8]

Hoover contrasted the false liberalism of the New Deal with the true liberalism represented in the Constitution. In 1935, he urged the abolition of the National Recovery Act, saying it was the equivalent of fascist regimentation and an abandonment of "the principles of real social justice upon which this Nation was founded." Hoover concluded that the act violated the spirit and letter of the Constitution, which was the cornerstone of his own philosophy and which secured the blessings of liberty on the exceptional American System.

In almost every respect, the Hoover-Roosevelt debate over equality and liberty parallels the conservative-liberal argument today. Roosevelt felt that, in the wake of an economic crisis, it was time to focus attention on what economic forces had done to the forgotten man. And this, he argued, could only be accomplished by greater market regulation by government and, ultimately, higher taxes on the wealthy. Hoover, in turn, argued that such government intervention was not needed, that there was capacity within the American System to self-correct, and that such permanent changes would substitute for America's liberty the kind of economic regimentation being pursued in the planned economies of Europe. As we shall see, that debate, in more or less those same terms, is on the front burner of public policy today.

OBAMA AND INCOME INEQUALITY

In a series of speeches that began during his 2012 presidential campaign, and culminated in his 2013 second inaugural address, President Barack Obama sought to make income equality "the defining issue of our time." When he first raised it in a significant

8. This paragraph and the next paragraph rely heavily on Hoover, *The Challenge to Liberty,* 76, 115, 126, 203. See also Hoover, *Addresses Upon the American Road,* 46–47.

way, in a December 6, 2011, campaign speech in Osawatomie, Kansas, it seemed like a clever attempt to turn attention away from the underperformance of the economy and toward inequality as the crucial economic issue of the day. Obama pointed out the rise in income of the very wealthy, while middle-class families struggled to keep up, asserting that we had a level of inequality not seen since the Great Depression. His call to action was to reexamine the tax system, arguing that America could not afford the level of support needed for education and manufacturing while continuing "tax breaks for the wealthiest Americans." Later, he added a major increase to the minimum wage as another piece of the solution.

Expanding his attack on business and the wealthy, Obama gave his famous "you didn't build that" speech in Roanoke, Virginia, on July 13, 2012. His argument was that people who thought they had succeeded by taking advantage of opportunities and hard work were mistaken because "you didn't get there on your own." Citing government's role in building bridges, roads, the Internet, and infrastructure generally, he said if you had a successful business, "you didn't build that either." He was widely criticized for minimizing the individual work ethic and the free enterprise system, but he pressed on. In his second inaugural address, Obama said: "For we, the people, understand that our country cannot succeed when a shrinking few do very well and a growing many barely make it." He defended entitlement programs as part of the support that allows Americans to take risks and "make this country great." And so Obama aligned himself with Roosevelt and the progressives, arguing that the issue was not so much growing the economy as it was distributing its gains fairly.

Obama in 2012 and 2013 echoed Franklin Roosevelt's attacks on the fat cats who weren't paying their fair share in the 1930s, a kind of presidential class warfare that really had not been seen since that time. And, like Roosevelt, Obama also called for higher tax rates on the wealthy to ameliorate the problem. Some argue that Obama has long had a redistributionist agenda, citing a statement from his early days in politics: "I think the trick is figuring out how do we structure government systems that pool resources and hence facilitate some redistribution—because I actually believe in redistribution, at least at a certain level to make sure that everybody's got a shot."[9] Obama has stayed the course early in his second term, insisting that he would not agree to any solution to the "fiscal cliff" and budgetary sequestration problems of early 2013 that did not include higher marginal tax rates for top income earners, resulting in the first tax rate increase in twenty years.

President Obama's attention to income inequality has become the next round in the age-old battle between liberty and equality. To what extent is income inequality a legitimate concern of government? Is income inequality an economic problem, or is it primarily a social question? How does one properly measure economic equality—that is to say, is income really the most appropriate indicator of economic equality, and is it being properly accounted for? Is taxing those with higher levels of income even more heavily a legitimate response for government to undertake, and one that is likely to have salutary economic and social effects? These are all questions raised by Obama's relentless focus on income inequality and his insistence upon greater tax inequality as the solution.

THE LIBERTY COUNTERPOINT: ECONOMIC DEPENDENCY

A memorable counterpoint in the income inequality debate also came during the 2012 presidential campaign when Mitt Romney's remarks about growing government dependency (which he later disavowed) made to a group of donors became public:

> There are 47 percent of the people who will vote for the president no matter what . . . who are dependent upon government, who believe

9. Susan Crabtree, "Republicans Point to Obama 'Redistribution' Video," *Washington Times,* September 18, 2012, http://www.washingtontimes.com/blog /inside-politics/2012/sep/18/republicans-point-obama-redistribution-video.

that they are victims. . . . These are people who pay no income tax. . . . I'll never convince them that they should take personal responsibility and care for their lives.[10]

Conventional wisdom held that Romney's remarks were politically damaging, but they nevertheless highlighted a large and growing problem: that more and more people are dependent upon government for financial support. And this dependency on government, which is damaging to personal liberty, will only increase as federal expenditures and entitlement spending increase.

This debate was joined in a powerful way by political economist Nicholas Eberstadt's 2012 book, *A Nation of Takers: America's Entitlement Epidemic.* He opens his book with a quotation from former Harvard professor and liberal US Senator Daniel Patrick Moynihan: "The issue of welfare is the issue of dependency. . . . To be poor is an objective condition; to be dependent, a subjective one as well." Eberstadt then develops a powerful case that the federal government has become essentially a wealth transfer and entitlements machine, to the detriment of the people and their government. By 2010, Eberstadt points out, entitlement spending had risen so dramatically that it constituted two-thirds of all federal spending, with everything else (defense, justice, and all other constitutional obligations) only making up one-third. Supporting at least part of Mitt Romney's 47 percent statement, Eberstadt says the United States is "on the verge of a symbolic threshold: the point at which more than half of all American households receive, and accept, transfer payments from the government." Census Bureau data placed that number at just over 49 percent by early 2011.[11]

---

10. Seema Mehta, "Romney slams Obama backers as dependent on government, tax dodgers," *Los Angeles Times,* September 17, 2012, http://articles.latimes.com/2012/sep/17/news/la-pn-romney-obama-supporters-victims-20120917.

11. Phil Izzo, "Number of the Week: Half of US Lives in Household Getting Government Benefits," *Real Time Economics* (blog), *Wall Street Journal,* May 26,

The implications of "a nation of takers" are profound, indeed. For one thing, a government heavily engaged in transferring money from those paying high taxes to others paying few if any taxes has developed a kind of Robin Hood, or even confiscatory, tax system. Some people are not just paying their fair share, they are actually transferring their wealth to others through the medium of government. To increase both the tax rates, as President Obama has done and says he will continue to do, and the volume of entitlements, which is inevitable as the baby boomer generation ages, is creating a very different government and society than has ever been contemplated before in the United States. It is no longer about equality of opportunity; it is about equalizing income through taxes and transfers. This has come about so rapidly that the moral and even political case for this transformation has not been carefully considered.

And what about the social consequences of "a nation of takers"? There are now people who receive government benefits from before birth to death. In one of his 2012 campaign commercials, Barack Obama showed "Julia," who received the benefit of government transfers from preschool to health care to small business loans and retirement. As Eberstadt points out in his book, "The habituation of Americans to life on entitlement benefits has already progressed much further than any of us might realize," noting that, as of 2009, 45 percent of American children under 18 were receiving some form of means-tested government assistance.

INCOME INEQUALITY AND THE GOVERNMENT RESPONSE

At the base of the income inequality debate are two fundamental questions, one about the age-old question of liberty versus equality and one about the proper role of government. If we were founded

---

2012. http://blogs.wsj.com/economics/2012/05/26/number-of-the-week
-half-of-u-s-lives-in-household-getting-benefits.

as a nation committed to individual freedom and to allowing people to pursue happiness each in his or her own way, isn't income equality a bridge too far? Shouldn't the right question be about equality of opportunity, and isn't income equality really a question about equality of monetary outcome? And in this whole matter of economic or financial inequality, is it the proper role of government to become, in effect, a transfer agent, moving wealth from one social class to another through its system of taxation? To these fundamental questions we now turn.

If we live in a society premised on individual freedom and equality of opportunity, is income equality the right question to ask, or the right measure to pursue? Put succinctly, income inequality should only be a policy problem in a free society if an individual's income is permanent or static. If, on the other hand, people are able to move from, say, the lower-income quartile to a higher one, such an economy could be deemed healthy. Mobility within an economy is really the test of a free society, rather than the dollar difference in income levels between one quartile and another. Indeed, growth at the top may well represent a dynamic and entrepreneurial economy, with lots of important developments leading to new, successful companies—the hallmark of the US economy for some time. Do we wish to penalize people like Bill Gates and Steve Jobs (and their investors) who have created not only new companies but entire new industries? The real equality question is whether people have an opportunity to move up or down the income scale, not the existence of different income levels or the size of the gaps between them. To put it another way, focusing on income inequality in a given year in an economy is really about equality of outcomes, not the equality of opportunity which is the hallmark of a free society.

Rather than looking at income inequality and its focus on equality of outcomes, we should be watching income mobility, which better measures equality of opportunity. A US Department of Treasury study, for example, looked at income mobility from 1996 to 2005 and concluded that, during the study period, over one-half of tax-payers moved to a different income quintile. Approximately one-half of taxpayers in the bottom income quintile in 1996 moved to a higher income group by 2005; of the top 0.01 percent of taxpayers in 1996, only 25 percent remained in the highest income category by 2005.[12] These results were consistent with a similar study of the period 1987–1996. As Mark Perry, professor of economics and finance at the University of Michigan, points out, trend data on income mobility tell us much more than statistical snapshots of income inequality. Our real concern should be whether income mobility slows or stops.[13]

There is also debate about the income equality data and their policy implications. By one commonly employed measure, with a scale of zero to one, income inequality in the United States is .469, compared with an average of .31 in Europe, a gap that is not terribly surprising given the historically distinctive philosophies about income and equality between the United States and Western Europe.[14] But, as several economists point out, typical measures of income for these purposes often leave out a number of sources of people's financial support such as government transfers to lower-income families and non-salary benefits to workers. In addition, the income inequality charts generally report data before taxes, ignoring the effect of our progressive income tax system. Using a definition of income equality that takes these factors into

12. US Department of Treasury, "Income Mobility in the US from 1996 to 2005," November 13, 2007 (revised March 2008).

13. Mark J. Perry, "Income inequality can be explained by demographics, and because the demographics change, there's income mobility," *Carpe Diem* (blog), January 7, 2013, http://www.aei-ideas.org/2013/01/income-inequality-can-be -explained-by-demographics-and-because-the-demographics-change-theres -income-mobility.

14. Kip Hagopian and Lee Ohanian, "The Mismeasure of Inequality," Hoover.org, *Policy Review* No. 174, August 1, 2012, http://www.hoover.org /publications/policy-review/article/123566.

account, income inequality in the United States actually declined in the period between 1993 and 2009.[15] Further, most charts of income inequality use small increments of measurement until they reach $250,000 or so, and then lump everyone else into a single "rich" bucket. If, instead, you continued to chart the smaller increments, there is no massive growth at the top but rather a continuing distribution of people in all the income groupings. So it seems misguided, without much more study, to draw conclusions about the extent of income inequality and to begin changing tax policy to remedy it.

It is quite a leap to conclude, as President Obama has, that a compelling solution to the "problem" of income inequality is a dramatic change in tax rates. Such an approach ignores that the US income tax is already highly progressive. In a study by the Organisation for Economic Cooperation and Development in 2008, the US tax rate was the most progressive—22 percent higher than the average of the twenty-four countries (including the wealthiest countries in Europe, among others)—of the countries studied.[16] Still, President Obama has advanced his "Buffett rule" approach, requiring that the wealthy pay a minimum of 30 percent on all their income. Besides taking the progressive nature of US tax policy even further, this approach (named after Warren Buffett) ignores that a great deal of wealthy taxpayers' income comes from investments, which are generally taxed already at the corporate level and which generate growth and jobs. But with the leading income inequality economists arguing for top tax rates of 50 percent, or even 70 percent or 90 percent, these ideas are likely to be pressed further.

The income inequality case seems far too weak to lead to the conclusion that tax rates should undergo significant change, espe-

15. Ibid.
16. Ibid.

cially when US tax rates are already highly progressive. And such an approach only accelerates the dangerous trend of fewer people funding government and of the growth of the government wealth transfer enterprise. If nothing else, it should be clear that this is part of a determined effort to move America more toward equality of outcomes, with less focus on equality of opportunity.

OBAMACARE: EQUALITY VERSUS LIBERTY

President Obama's signature legislative accomplishment, health care reform, is another example of a shift away from liberty and toward equality. As Alexis de Tocqueville observed in his classic *Democracy in America,* a fundamental difference between the French and American revolutions was the French emphasis on equality and the American focus on liberty. In fact, Tocqueville's view was that the French, with their "liberté, equalité, et fraternité," were so enamored of equality that they would choose to be equal in slavery rather than unequal in freedom. In many ways, this nineteenth-century observation raises the fundamental question of American political philosophy over the last 150 years: the liberty narrative, emphasizing equality of opportunity and a limited role for government, versus the equality narrative, arguing for equality of outcome and favoring government limitations on free markets and individual liberty in order to institutionalize equality.

In fact, the Hoover-Roosevelt debate conjures up two classic caricatures—the rugged individual and the forgotten man—that personify the liberty and equality health care narratives. When the present health care structure was created during President Lyndon Johnson's "Great Society" of the 1960s, Medicare and Medicaid took care of the forgotten man while employer-employee health insurance programs covered the health care of the rugged individual. Thus a political compromise between the two narratives allowed health care policy to move forward. Later, first lady Hillary Clinton led the charge for universal health care in 1993. Her plan would have imposed a mandatory, universal health care insurance requirement administered by a massive government bureaucracy. The plan fizzled out in Congress and helped usher in the Newt Gingrich revolution against big government in the midterm elections of 1994.

From a policy point of view, it seemed odd then that President Obama, in the face of polls showing that 84 percent of Americans were satisfied with their health coverage, selected a massive overhaul that changed the entire system. Wouldn't history suggest that addressing the problems for the 16 percent would make more sense than tackling the whole with a comprehensive government plan? In the early going, Obama seemed quite clear that, to him, the health care matter was a moral question, not merely a political or economic one. He accused his opponents, in strikingly biblical language, of "bearing false witness." He argued for his plan on the grounds that "I am my brother's keeper, I am my sister's keeper," adding that this is a moral conviction going to the "heart of who we are as a people." Rather than Johnson's more pragmatic and balanced approach, this was an all-or-nothing moral crusade.

Less apparent, but nevertheless real, are the moral arguments of the liberty narrative. Individual freedom, even a decision whether to have health care, is one. Government control over individuals and markets is another. Cost and competition are also fundamental. True, it is costly to be free, but that choice belongs to the individual, not the government. And, the liberty narrative argues, the only way we will improve health care is through competition, not protectionism or a government takeover. All these arguments lost out, however, in a party-line vote to add yet one more expensive government entitlement program on a scale not seen since Roosevelt's New Deal and Johnson's Great Society, pushing America's political pendulum ever closer to the European equality narrative and away from liberty.

CONCLUSION: REPLACE THE LIBERTY BELL WITH THE EQUALITY BELL?

For both economic and philosophical reasons, it is time to bring down the curtain on the New Deal, rather than continue to cultivate and extend it. Surely the massive government debt, and its projected rise as the baby boomers become eligible for further entitlements, has demonstrated that the New Deal is not sustainable. And yet, rather than reject the New Deal, or at least curtail it or bring it under some discipline, President Obama chooses to extend and accelerate it. The income inequality debates and increases in tax rates on the wealthy are pages right out of the New Deal playbook. Pushing through a complete overhaul, and virtual government takeover, of health care adds yet further entitlements to the mountain of debt.

New York Times columnist David Brooks caught this "collectivist" spirit in President Obama's second inaugural address, a message Brooks felt was essentially a rejection of individualism and a call to collective action. But Brooks would contrast this moment with the earlier New Deal and Great Society, whose "laws were enacted when America was still a young and growing nation." At this stage of our history, however, Brooks points out that "we are now a mature nation with an aging population. Far from being under-institutionalized, we are bogged down with a bloated political system, a tangled tax code, a byzantine legal code, and a crushing debt."[17] It is time to bury the New Deal, not to praise it or extend it. But this may only happen out of economic necessity, when the debt crisis finally hits a moment when it can no longer be patched over, when the fiscal can may no longer be kicked down the road. Perhaps only then will America be forced to face the reality that the New Deal era of eighty years needs to draw to a close, to be

17. David Brooks, "The Collective Turn," *New York Times,* January 21, 2013, A25.

replaced by greater attention to fiscal responsibility and a return to the liberty narrative.

Otherwise, we are forced to conclude that the real agenda of both Roosevelt's New Deal and Obama's policies was not so much to address an economic crisis as it was to use the short-term crisis to accomplish a long-term, redistributionist social agenda. As Rahm Emanuel famously said: "You never want a serious crisis to go to waste. And what I mean by that is an opportunity to do things you think you could not do before."

At this rate, America is on the road to replacing its Liberty Bell with an equality bell. Harvard political philosopher Harvey Mansfield points out that this is always the temptation for democracy: to love liberty but to love equality more, and to exaggerate itself and go too far. "In demanding equality it tries to level differences, claiming to raise the low but often actually lowering the high," Mansfield says.[18] Conservatism needs to stand for liberty and for equality of opportunity against this progressive agenda of economic redistribution and social equality of outcomes.

18. "What Is the Future of Conservatism in the Wake of the 2012 Election?—A Symposium," *Commentary Magazine*, January 2013, 34.

CHAPTER 3

Limited Government versus Expansive Government

From the beginning, limited government has been part of the American agenda. When the Declaration of Independence issued its complaints against King George III for establishing his tyranny over the colonies, among the bill of particulars was that "He has erected a multitude of New Offices, and sent hither swarms of Officers to harass our people, and eat out their substance." By the time of the New Deal, our own growing and intrusive federal government had become a concern articulated by Herbert Hoover, and it is at the very heart of today's debate about government spending and the federal budget deficit which threaten to "eat out [our] substance." In fact, one of the stark contrasts in the 2012 presidential campaign was between Republican vice presidential candidate Paul Ryan, who constantly reminded voters that we have the largest deficit and federal government since World War II, and Barack Obama, who favored growing government infrastructure and spending to enable public sector growth to lead America out of the recession.

Roosevelt's 1932 Campaign Speeches: The Case for Activist Government

Throughout his 1932 campaign speeches, Roosevelt sought to establish the need for a much larger role for the federal government in the wake of the Great Depression. In his "Forgotten Man" radio address, delivered on April 7, 1932, Roosevelt declared, "In my calm judgment, the nation faces today a more grave emergency than in 1917. . . . These unhappy times call for the building of plans that rest upon . . . the forgotten man at the bottom of the economic pyramid." There is, out there, "an emergency at least equal to that of war. Let us mobilize to meet it." These images—the forgotten man, emergency, war, mobilization—would continue to characterize Roosevelt's New Deal and his rhetorical defense of it.

The military imagery continued in his first inaugural address: ". . . we must move as a trained and loyal army willing to sacrifice for the good of a common discipline, because without such discipline no progress is made, no leadership becomes effective." And such a view, he acknowledged, brought with it significant constitutional consequences. "It is to be hoped," he said, that the constitutional separation of powers will be "wholly adequate to meet the unprecedented task before us." But if not, then, in accordance with "my constitutional duty . . . I shall ask the Congress for the one remaining instrument to meet the crisis: broad executive power to wage a war against the emergency, as great as the power that would be given to me if we were in fact invaded by a foreign foe."

Roosevelt's Commonwealth Club Address of September 23, 1932, raised a marker, advancing a fundamental philosophical and chronological change from an older to a newer American order of things. Roosevelt admitted that, long ago, Jeffersonian individualism, supported by cheap land, made sense as a defensible way of life. But that world is over, he said. We have been dealing with the Machine

Age lately and the unscrupulous work of a few "financial titans." The implications of this, he said, are clear: ". . . equality of opportunity as we have known it no longer exists. Our industrial plant is built; the problem just now is whether under existing conditions it is not overbuilt. Our last frontier has long since been reached, and there is practically no more free land." He concluded with the prediction that we are "steering a steady course toward economic oligarchy" if we follow the old, worn-out, do-nothing, laissez faire of the last ten years of Hoover as secretary of commerce and then president. At the heart of the Roosevelt critique was, first, that Hoover's rugged individualism, or American Individualism, is no more than a fancy name for narrow individual self-interest and, second, that Hoover's "constructive government" is a euphemism for a do-nothing government.

HOOVER'S CASE FOR CONSTRUCTIVE, NOT DESTRUCTIVE, GOVERNMENT

As Roosevelt's New Deal began to be implemented in 1933, Hoover became alarmed by the growth in federal power, budgets, employment, rules, deficits, and, most importantly, the use to which these increased federal activities were put. With the dramatic growth in public works projects and the creation of dozens of new federal agencies, the modern debate about the size and scope of government was launched during the New Deal era. Before the Great Depression, federal expenditures were relatively small, accounting for about 3 percent of gross national product (GNP).[1] By the end of the century, that figure exceeded 20 percent. Certainly, in relative terms, there was significant growth in government during the

---

1. David M. Kennedy, *Freedom from Fear: The American People in Depression and War, 1929–1945* (New York: Oxford University Press, 1999), 55.

Roosevelt years: he nearly doubled the federal budget during his first term alone.[2] Hoover claimed in a 1938 speech that Roosevelt had also doubled the national debt (either direct or guaranteed) from $21 billion to $42 billion.[3]

But it is in Hoover's attention to the qualitative danger to core American values, and not simply in the increased quantity of federal activity, that we can discern the roots of modern American conservatism. Hoover's was the prophetic conservative voice in the wilderness at the height of New Deal progressivism, pointing away from the vast growth in federal power and its debilitating effects on American individualism and values and toward the ideas of limited government, equality of opportunity, and constitutional federalism that conservatives advance today. Indeed, with the many parallels between the economy and the role of government in the Roosevelt and Obama eras, Hoover's words seem especially contemporary, right down to the unresolved problems of entitlement spending and public pensions.

Hoover's understanding of core American values was initially expressed in the 1920s and is best summarized as combining "constructive government" with an enduring commitment to "rugged individualism." Constructive government, to Hoover's way of thinking, was a set of ideas and practices about how the federal government should interact with the private sector in a time of postwar reconstruction and industrial and economic development. Constructive government was hardly the vast bureaucracy later created by the New Deal and the Great Society, nor was it a non-caring, laissez faire, do-nothing approach as rather cheaply portrayed by the Roosevelt administration and progressive historians. Instead it

---

2. Amity Shlaes, *The Forgotten Man: A New History of the Great Depression* (New York: Harper Collins Publishers, 2007), 391.

3. Associated Press, "Hoover Warns New Deal Leads US to Fascism," *Washington Post,* May 6, 1938.

sought to articulate the proper role for government within the larger context of equality of opportunity and individual freedom.

"According to my social theories," Hoover said, "any organization by citizens for their own welfare is preferable to the same action by government." He would later distinguish his approach to constructive government with the "sheer economic fascism" of the New Deal, noting that demands for government action to fix prices, wages, production, and distribution were "no less an invasion of liberty than Socialism."[4] To Hoover, the line between constructive action by the government and destructive government control was clear and, in terms of conservative values, one he could not cross.

In his November 2, 1928, "constructive government" speech, Hoover reiterated the exceptionalism of the American order. The Founders, he said, put in place a unique political, social, and economic system. In addition to creating what he called a great system of political self-government, they instituted "a revolutionary social system," based on the ideal of equal opportunity, and a new economic system in which capital and labor, by joint effort, have "laid away the old theory of inevitable poverty." But the main point of this speech was to indicate "the three potential fields in which the principles and impulses of our American System *require* that government take constructive action." He justified the leadership role of government in these three fields because "they comprise those activities which no local community can itself assume and which the individual initiative and enterprise of our people cannot wholly compass."

These three essential activities of constructive government for Hoover encompass public works; public education and public health; and social and economic cooperation. At first glance, these constructive activities seem to cover a wide range of what today we would recognize as a larger role for the federal government to play than as a mere "referee" of the system, as some conservatives would

4. Hoover, *Memoirs*, 62–63, 174.

prefer. But Hoover's larger purpose was to pursue a model whereby government, business, and labor work together constructively in a joint effort of reconstruction after World War I within a harmonious American System. There is no understanding of government as the owner of the system.[5]

Presidential leadership for Hoover meant being guider in chief rather than commander in chief. Consequently, as president he called a meeting of professors, seeking to recruit the best brains in the country to compile sets of new data that would serve as the foundation for his future public policy.

HOOVER'S CASE FOR AMERICAN INDIVIDUALISM, NOT EUROPEAN PATERNALISM

If constructive government was the pragmatic side of Hoover's political philosophy, then American individualism constituted its reflective side. Hoover set forth the essence of it in a 1922 pamphlet, intended as a commencement address but never delivered, called *American Individualism*. At the time of its publication, the *New York Times Book Review* described it as one of the "few great formulations of American political theory." Fredrick Jackson Turner, the influential author of the "Frontier Thesis," said it "contains the New and Old Testament of the American gospel."[6]

5. Amity Shlaes has argued that his active support for these very government activities demonstrates that Hoover actually laid the foundation for the New Deal, since he made it easier for Roosevelt to expand the size of the federal government. Our research indicates that Hoover increased the size of the government far less than claimed by the libertarian right and he certainly did not use the money to transform the American System. Shlaes is correct: the roots of American conservatism are planted in pre-WWII America. But the question is: how far back should one travel to discover these roots? Shlaes takes us back to Calvin Coolidge and his resistance to the Progressive movement. See Shlaes, *The Forgotten Man*, and also *Coolidge* (New York: Harper Collins Publishers, 2013).

6. Margaret Hoover, *American Individualism: How a New Generation of Conservatives Can Save the Republican Party* (New York: Crown Forum, 2011), 12.

The word "American" is central to this essay and to Hoover's own political philosophy. Having spent so much of his career abroad, especially conducting postwar relief efforts in Europe, Hoover returned, as many expatriates do, with a deeper appreciation for America and its values. Hoover came home to the United States so enamored of its way of life relative to Europe that his values were American first, conservative second. In fact, he framed his essay by setting his *American individualism* against the other great social philosophies or "isms" of the day, all of which had a strong Old World collectivist or anarchist character. As he said, his faith in the American System was "confirmed and deepened by the searching experiences of seven years of service in the backwash and misery of war."

Hoover's understanding of individualism in this essay, however, and in his own personal philosophy is not the uncaring and self-ish rugged individualism with which he later became associated. In fact, it is quite the opposite: it is a communal and cooperative exer-cise of individualism, based on the notion of voluntary service to others. It was not a rugged individualism that ignored others; it was rugged in the sense that it came from the pioneers of the American frontier.

Hoover actually sought a balance between concern for oneself—an "individual initiative" that spurs economic progress—and a concern for the community that produces human decency. We suggest that what Hoover meant by rugged individualism, or what he elsewhere called "spiritual individualism," is similar to what Tocqueville meant by self-interest, rightly understood. Both emphasized the importance of voluntary cooperation and both saw the paternalistic state, or the dependent individual, as a danger to ordered liberty. Hoover's idea of rugged individualism, then, is compatible with the ideal of community service, civic engage-ment, and a "sense of mutuality" with the community at large. Hoover's American individualism is based, as he says, on equality of opportunity, the "fair chance" of Abraham Lincoln, the great emancipator.[7]

Hoover referred to the virtues of rugged individualism in his Madison Square Garden speech, delivered on October 22, 1928. This speech, however, should be read in light of the *American Individualism* essay and his practice of constructive government. In New York, Hoover summarized the challenge of reconstruction in the 1920s:

> We were challenged by a peace-time choice between the American System of rugged individualism and a European philosophy of diametrically opposed doctrines—doctrines of paternalism and state socialism. The acceptance of these ideas would have meant the destruction of self-government. . . . It would have meant the undermining of the individual initiative and enterprise through which our people have grown to incomparable greatness.

Lest his rugged individualism remark be misunderstood, he said that the United States is not, nor should it be, "free-for-all and devil-take-the-hindmost. The very essence of equality of opportunity and of American individualism is that there shall be no domination by any group or combination in this republic, whether it be business or political. . . . It is no system of laissez faire," Hoover said.

Hoover's Madison Square Garden Speech of October 31, 1932, was his pre-election response to Roosevelt's Commonwealth Club Speech. Said Hoover, "We are told by the opposition that we must have a change, that we must have a new deal. It is not the change that comes from normal development of national life to which I object, but the proposal to alter the whole foundations of our national life which have been builded through generations of testing and struggle, and of the principles upon which we have builded the nation."

7. Lloyd, ed., *The Two Faces of Liberalism,* 33.

In the end, Hoover advocated for an American System that he described as "peculiar to the American people."[8] Foreshadowing modern American conservative philosophies, Hoover understood that "it is founded on a peculiar conception of self-government designed to maintain the equal opportunity of the individual, and through decentralization it brings about and maintains these responsibilities. The centralization of government will undermine responsibilities and will destroy the system." This is why Hoover concluded that "this campaign . . . is a contest between two philosophies of government." In Hoover's view, the New Deal proposals "represent a radical departure from the foundations of 150 years which have made this the greatest nation in the world," which means that the 1932 election would decide "the direction our nation will take over a century to come."[9] We see emerging a very different brand of conservatism in Herbert Hoover, one much more vocal and strident, as he saw American values coming under attack. There would be no middle way, only a striking choice that Hoover saw more clearly and articulated more directly than anyone else of his time.

THE FUNDAMENTAL SOUNDNESS OF THE AMERICAN SYSTEM

Hoover's most persistent argument against the political economy of the New Deal was that it took as its central premise that there was something systemically wrong with the American regime. Nor did he approve of the permanently enhanced role for government emanating out of the European experience of the 1920s. Hoover saw the cause and continuation of the Great Depression in America to be the inability of Europe to secure a healthy political, social, and economic postwar recovery and reconstruction. In his final message as the president to Congress, he stated that "our major difficulties

8. Ibid., 127.
9. Ibid., 138.

find their origins in the economic weakness of foreign nations." This fact, he said, was so self-evident that it "requires no demonstration."

What else should the federal government do in the face of this unprecedented economic situation? One swift answer: do not abandon the course of American values. Hoover believed that government should aid the recovery process by constraining the federal government deficit, restraining government expenditures, and eliminating waste by reorganizing government departments. He also recommended "extensive cooperative measures" in the private and local sectors as well as the unprecedented acceleration and expansion of such federal public works as "public building, harbor, flood control, highway, waterway, aviation, merchant and naval ship construction" already on the books in 1928–1929.[10]

None of these programs is inconsistent with the American System of limited government. Finally, Hoover said, the government must make sure that every act of government conformed to "a complete philosophy of the people's purposes and destiny. Ours is a distinctive government with a unique history and background, consciously dedicated to specific ideals of liberty and to a faith in the inviolable sanctity of the individual human spirit." Hoover did attempt, certainly initially, to address the economic crisis within his constructive government framework, focusing on voluntarism and collaboration among government, labor, and business. When Hoover did intervene in the economy, he did so, as historian Amity Shlaes acknowledges, as a "constitutionalist . . . within the rules."[11]

In *The Memoirs of Herbert Hoover: The Great Depression, 1929–1941,* Hoover identified the election of 1932 as "a turning point in American life—and possibly the world." It attempted to transform America and revolutionize the world. The whole purpose of the New Deal, he said, was to make America over, and this involved

10. Ibid., 41.

11. Shlaes, *The Forgotten Man,* 6.

an alteration in American values and a collectivist reading of the Constitution. "No president should undermine the independence of the legislative and judicial branches by seeking to discredit them," Hoover wrote. "The constitutional division of powers is the bastion of our liberties and was not designed as a battleground to display the prowess of presidents."

LIMITED GOVERNMENT TODAY

Seventy-five years later, the question of expansion of the federal government by progressives versus limited government espoused by conservatives continues to be a central issue. But there are several ways to define "limited government." One way to understand limited government is essentially quantitative, seeking to measure the sheer size of government: the number of federal employees and departments, the amount of government spending, government spending as a percentage of gross domestic product, and so forth. But a second approach is more qualitative in nature, examining people's dependency on government, the extent of its reach into daily life and individual liberty, the growth of the regulatory state, and the balance of federal/state/local power. With the sheer size of the federal government relatively modest in his day, Herbert Hoover's concern was more about the latter. But today, when conservatives speak of limited government, they are concerned about both its size and its impact.

GOVERNMENT KEEPS GROWING IN SIZE

One widely accepted way of measuring the relative size of government is to identify the share of gross domestic product (GDP) constituted by federal spending. This figure was around 2 to 3 percent from the Founding through the New Deal, except for significant spikes during wartime (approximately 15 percent during the Civil

War and 23 percent during World War I). Then, beginning with the New Deal, the figure grew steadily to 20 percent and spiked during World War II at 41.5 percent. Government spending dropped following the war but then resumed its steady rise, dropping some during the peace dividend years of the 1980s and 1990s, but rising again now to around 25 percent. Projections that include expected growth in entitlements show the number growing dramatically higher in the coming decades. Clearly, there was a sea change in government spending during the New Deal which continues and accelerates today.

Tightening the focus to more recent times, when the debate about big government became more intense, the government spending-to-GDP comparisons fluctuated within a relatively narrow range, at least until 2008. During the last three decades, the figure has ranged from a low of 18 percent to a high of 25 percent, with the thirty-five-year average at 21 percent. Of course, some of the rise in recent years has been caused by the underperforming economy against which government spending is measured. Still, with limited economic growth potentially a longer-term norm, and with the expected major growth in entitlements, this measure of government size is of real concern for decades to come.

Another quantitative approach to the big government question might be to examine the number of federal employees, in particular nonmilitary employees—since, as we saw in the federal spending figures, wartime creates anomalies in the numbers. Again the figures are mixed, showing relatively modest changes (some increases, some reductions) from year to year. In contrast to total spending, which has grown dramatically, federal civilian employment was actually slightly lower in 2008 than in 1978. But both the number of federal employees and the payroll are on the rise during the current Obama administration.

Yet another quantitative approach would be to measure the volume of federal regulations imposed upon the people at any time.

Funding for federal regulatory agencies is at an all-time high, as is the number of their employees. The number of pages in the Federal Register with new rules is also at a record high. The only president who reduced federal regulatory outlays in the past thirty-five years was Ronald Reagan in his first term, though growth in Clinton's first term was modest. Government issuance of new regulations has generally grown between minus 13 percent (Reagan's first term) to 9.66 percent in George W. Bush's second term. But President Obama is setting a record pace at over 41 percent.

The modern quantitative narrative doesn't necessarily track by political party. For example, the largest recent reductions in federal spending compared to GDP and in federal civilian employment both occurred under President Clinton. But, again, the most alarming growth of the past thirty-five years appears to be taking place right now and into the future, with baby boomers reaching retirement age. Cost increases in entitlements such as Medicare, Social Security, and now Obamacare (the Patient Protection and Affordable Care Act) look frightening. Congressman Paul Ryan was certainly not wrong when he said, during the 2012 presidential campaign, that the federal debt and the federal government have never been larger. But overall the changes in federal spending and employment from 1977–2008 are a mixed picture, with ups and downs throughout the period.

THE GROWING GOVERNMENT ROLE

Perhaps, as Hoover Institution Senior Fellow Peter Berkowitz asserts, the real argument is not about big government, as a matter of size, but about limiting government and the role it plays in our society as well as in our individual lives.[12] Here, unlike the up-and-down

12. Peter Berkowitz, *Constitutional Conservatism: Liberty, Self-Government, and Political Moderation* (Stanford, CA: Hoover Institution Press, 2013).

data about the size of government, all measures point to steady and significant growth in the role and impact of the federal government from the New Deal to the present.

For example, Herbert Hoover was deeply concerned about the unhealthy sense of dependency on government that develops when it plays a dominant role in society. Mitt Romney attempted to address this to a group of donors in the 2012 campaign, in a way that wasn't artful but that raised a serious point, when he said that 47 percent of Americans pay no federal taxes and are therefore dependent on the government. The nonpartisan Tax Policy Center confirmed that, as of July 2011, 46.4 percent of Americans, or 76 million individuals or families, paid no federal income taxes in 2011.[13] Of course many of these had low-income jobs and paid other taxes, so concluding they are "dependent" on government is not entirely accurate. But this dependency problem will grow dramatically when baby boomers go on Social Security and Medicare. Thirty years ago, 30 percent of American households received government assistance; now the number is nearly 50 percent and will easily surpass that number when Obamacare is implemented.

We hear a lot about rising income inequality (see chapter 2), but tax inequality seems like a potentially bigger problem if and when we reach the stage that half or more Americans pay no income tax and are living on government entitlements. Conservative political philosopher Harvey Mansfield sees the modern dependency problem, as Herbert Hoover did, in European terms. Speaking of the 2012 election, Mansfield said: "We now have an American political party and a European one." Americans ultimately voted, as Mansfield observed, "for dependency, for lack of ambition and for insolvency."[14]

13. See Tax Topics, Tax Policy Center (Urban Institute and Brookings Institution), http://www.taxpolicycenter.org/taxtopics/federal-taxes -households.cfm.

14. Sohrab Ahmari, "The Crisis of American Self-Government," *Wall Street Journal*, December 1, 2012, A13.

Another way to look at unlimited government is through the number of policy areas that are becoming federalized over time. Take K–12 education, for example, which has long been cited as the quintessential state and local matter. As recently as 1996, the Republican Party platform asserted that the federal Department of Education should be eliminated because there is no proper constitutional role for the federal government in education. But in the last fifteen years or so, K–12 education has been federalized to an astonishing degree, by Republicans and Democrats alike. First, former governors Clinton and Bush, who had pursued improved K–12 education in their respective states, came to the White House and began pushing for more federal spending and solutions in literacy and in K–12 education. Then Bush's No Child Left Behind Act began to set federal standards and establish testing schemes, followed soon enough by Obama's Race to the Top grants. Rather than mandating that states follow federal policy, the feds essentially bribed cash-starved states and school districts with substantial grants if they followed federal policy, a practice the Supreme Court criticized in the Medicaid portion of its 2012 ruling on the Affordable Care Act. Today, educators would say that the federal government is the most important player in education policy and reform, a far cry from where we were just a decade ago.

Similar changes are taking place across the board. Health care, for example, is not an enumerated power of the federal government, falling instead in the general welfare constitutional portfolio that is left to states. But just as we had huge problems in education, the underinsured population allowed the federal government to declare a crisis and justified its taking action that, again, shifts the major policy action from states to Washington, D.C. The same thing happens with environmental policy, climate change, drugs, and so on. The federal government has a consistent pattern of discovering a major national problem, declaring war on it, and then federalizing it, with the result that the federal government takes over more and more of the policy realm, depriving states of their constitutional powers and the people of their individual liberty.

RECENT HISTORY: THE PENDULUM SWINGS FURTHER LEFT THAN RIGHT

After the large rise in federal power during the New Deal, the next major development occurred during Lyndon Johnson's "Great Society." In fact, it is sometimes said that President Johnson's goal was, if possible, to out-Roosevelt Roosevelt. In Johnson's major address at the University of Michigan in 1964, he boldly proclaimed the "opportunity to move not only toward the rich society and the powerful society, but upward to the Great Society." He continued with a series of promises: "The Great Society rests on abundance and liberty for all. It demands an end to poverty and racial injustice, to which we are totally committed in our time. But that is just the beginning." The Great Society established Medicare and Medicaid, gave the first general federal aid to public schools, and so on.

In fact, Johnson's reach exceeded his grasp. Poverty, of course, was not eliminated and the Office of Economic Opportunity that led the war against it was eliminated in the next decade. But Medicare and Medicaid lived on and grew as major new planks of the federal entitlements platform. Twenty years later, Charles Murray, in his book *Losing Ground: American Social Policy, 1950–1980,* would argue that the Great Society's anti-poverty programs actually abetted rather than ameliorated it. And Joseph A. Califano Jr., Johnson's chief domestic policy adviser, would look back on this time and acknowledge that "the Government simply got into too many nooks and crannies of American life."[15] Hoover, who preached precisely

---

15. David E. Rosenbaum, "20 Years Later the Great Society Flourishes," *New York Times,* April 17, 1985, http://www.nytimes.com/1985/04/17/us/20-years-later -the-great-society-flourishes.html?pagewanted=all.

this message about Roosevelt's New Deal, would not have been as surprised as Califano.

On the other end of the spectrum of modern American presidents would be Ronald Reagan who, like Hoover, saw the dangers of growing federal power and not only spoke against it but, as president, took action to limit it. Reagan's signature political speech, "A Time for Choosing," in 1964, catalogued the sins of big government: high taxes, unbalanced budgets, government takeover of farming, dilution of private property rights. We can't solve our problems through more government and government planning, he said. In the 1980s as president, Reagan did cut government spending, tax rates, and federal regulations. Although all this took government back to its size of a decade earlier, the reductions were only temporary and big government marched on. This is the problem: government grows steadily, sometimes dramatically, for decades, and then one president tries to trim it, but ultimately only slows the long-term rate of increase.

Clearly, the Obama years are another New Deal and Great Society time of major government growth, both quantitatively and qualitatively. Due to Obama's aggressive takeover of health care, the rise in federal spending as a percentage of GDP, the dramatic growth in government regulations, and the baby boomer generation reaching Social Security and Medicare ages, it is time to sound an alarm. This, of course, the Tea Party has tried to do, pointing out the growth and intrusiveness of government. The Republican Party has taken up efforts to limit increased taxes and federal spending, but so far with only limited success. Some conservatives, such as Berkowitz, say it's time for conservatives to acknowledge that the era of big government is here to stay, though he wisely couples that with a call to continue the pursuit of limited government. What a strange world we live in when Democrat Bill Clinton in the 1990s said the era of big government was over, backing that up with cuts, and Republicans ratcheted up spending and debt in the 2000s, now accelerated by Obama and the Democrats. Herbert Hoover himself foreshadowed the long-term problems when he said in a 1936 speech: "Blessed are the young, for they shall inherit the national debt."

ADDITIONAL CHALLENGES TODAY

One of the great strengths of the American regime is its system of federalism. Even after deciding whether a matter is a proper concern of government, there remain important questions about which level (federal, state, local) and which branch (legislative, executive, judicial) of government should properly take action. Two trends seem quite clear in this arena: there is less concern about the federal government taking over state and local powers, and there is a greater consolidation of power in the executive branch.

Sadly, in our view, both political parties seem less interested in federalism, especially when they hold the power in Washington, D.C. Republicans and Democrats alike have federalized more policy areas, whether it's the Democrats federalizing wars on poverty or taking over health care, or the Republicans with wars on drugs or taking over education. If traditionally state and local matters are now federal matters, one could reasonably ask: What is the purpose in having state governments? Have the states simply become one more unnecessary layer of middle management between Washington, D.C., and local government? With most markets now being national and even international in scale, is everything now a federal question? Are states merely coordinators and facilitators now, receiving grants from Washington and dispersing them to local areas?

Part of the conservative challenge for the future is to make afresh the case for the states. Keeping government closer to the people is part of it, with states better able to understand regional and local needs. Further, states have long been recognized as valuable laboratories for experimentation and policy development. Before Washington swoops in with its one-size-fits-all approach to regulation, it is helpful to try out health care experiments, for example, in the states. To go a step further, shouldn't conservatives also be comfortable with allowing certain social questions to be resolved at the state level? Is it really necessary for Kansas and Oregon, for example, to take the same approach to medicinal marijuana or even same-sex marriage? Wouldn't it have been preferable for the people and the states to wrestle with some of the difficult questions about abortion rather than have a Supreme Court mandate abruptly handed down? National markets make it necessary to undertake much of economic policy and regulation at a federal level, but must every state now look alike on all social matters? Of course, this would require conservatives to abstain from going to federal courts all the time, as their liberal neighbors do, to challenge state social policies they do not like. But restraint from the overuse of judicial and federal action should be a principle of modern American conservatism.

Another limited government challenge today is the increasing consolidation of power in the executive, an issue that was certainly a hallmark of Roosevelt's New Deal. One sign of this is President Obama's growing use of executive orders to initiate policies he is unable to get through a divided Congress. Although there is no real constitutional authority for executive orders, presidents have long allowed themselves this privilege in the name of "executing" laws Congress has already passed. But, as the Supreme Court told President Harry Truman when he attempted to use an executive order to place all steel factories under federal control, executive orders may not be used to make laws, but only to execute them. What is new is Obama's use of executive orders to initiate laws. He kicked off his immigration reform initiative with sweeping executive orders that altered the playing field, especially changing the rules for young immigrants whose parents brought them to the United States illegally as children. Again, in gun control, the president started his initiative with twenty-three executive orders, many of which went well beyond existing law.

Another consolidation in executive power is seen in President Obama's significant expansion of "czars" who wield power similar to that of cabinet officers but do not require Senate confirmation. Depending on how you count them, Obama has appointed a record number of czars—somewhere around thirty-eight—on a wide variety of matters from his car czar and green jobs czar to the more standard drug and Middle East policy czars. For sheer creativity, it's hard to beat the Asian carp czar who, despite his exercise of federal power, nevertheless could not bend these fish invading the Great Lakes to his will. Most of these are unelected and unconfirmed senior White House officials whose considerable power seems to be a clear end-run around the Constitution.

The progressives have their favorite level of government, the federal, as well as their favorite branch, the executive. Starting with President Woodrow Wilson and culminating in Roosevelt's New Deal, progressives saw government as a science, best carried out by expert regulators and central planners (now czars) in the executive branch. Power shifted from the legislature (which the Founders had seen as the strongest of the branches of government) to the executive and, later, the judiciary (seen by the Founders as the "least dangerous" of the branches of government). This transferred power away from the people and toward the "experts." This is precisely the progressive experiment President Obama has continued by increasing the power of the executive branch, even though there is precious little evidence over the decades that government is expert in any kind of planning or regulation, especially over economic markets.

This would seem to be an important challenge for modern American conservatism to address: what is the preferred level and branch of government? In order to strengthen federalism, conservatives ought to be great defenders of local and state power under the Tenth Amendment and ought to resist growth in federal power. Unfortunately they have not consistently done this in modern times. Tremendous growth in federal spending and debt, as well as a federalizing of education policy, for example, all occurred during the years when George W. Bush and the Republican Party were in charge. What is needed are more constitutional conservatives, who are less concerned with winning every policy issue at all costs (making everything a federal case) and more interested in strengthening state and local power at the expense of the federal government. States should again become laboratories for experimentation of limited government and individual liberty.

At the same time, conservatives should advocate for the strength of the legislature over the executive and the courts. In our public policy classes, we sometimes ask students, after they have read *The Federalist Papers,* which branch the Founders saw as the strongest to the weakest. Their answer is clear: legislative, executive, and, last, judicial. Then we ask how they would rank their power today. Some say the executive is the strongest, some the judiciary, but they nearly all rank the legislature last. Again, this is where principled conservatives should make a stand: it is the legislature that represents the people, and we should be cautious about shifting its power to the so-called experts in the executive and judicial branches. Again, this may require restraint on the part of conservatives. But they should be prepared to lose some short-term battles in order to make progress in this longer-term war. We need fewer social or Christian or national security or even fiscal conservatives and more constitutional conservatives who will defend limited government and individual freedom.

CHAPTER 4

Constitutional Conservatism versus Liberal Reinterpretation

Constitutional changes would be required to enable the sweeping reforms that Franklin Roosevelt's New Deal intended. These were not debated in the federal and state legislatures as constitutional amendments, as one might have expected. Instead, we find the debate taking place in a series of speeches by Roosevelt and Hoover.

ROOSEVELT'S FIRST INAUGURAL ADDRESS

Franklin Roosevelt's intoxicating first inaugural address famously began with his assertion that "the only thing we have to fear is fear itself." This statement summarizes the subtle shift in language from individual rights and liberties that frequent Herbert Hoover's writing to a language of communal responsibilities and freedoms that are familiar to Roosevelt's audience. Roosevelt's "freedom from fear" and "freedom from want" in his 1941 State of the Union Message are the culmination of a ten-year plan to ultimately shift the meaning of the Bill of Rights away from supporting limitations on the reach of the federal government to supporting—perhaps guaranteeing—an expansion of the reach of the federal government.

To begin the first inaugural address with the notion that the central leadership objective is to establish freedom from fear is to elevate the social over the political role of the federal government. Accordingly, the government henceforth was to be concerned with actively securing the general social welfare, and perhaps even eliminating the causes of faction, rather than serving as the neutral adjudicator of the collisions and collusions that occur among individuals and groups operating within what Madison in "Federalist 10" called "civilized societies." Whereas commentators largely stop their coverage of the first inaugural address with the "freedom from fear" remark, the bulk of the speech actually outlined the agenda that animated modern American conservatism.

Roosevelt continued one of his campaign themes, arguing the need for national planning based on the new realization of "our interdependence on each other." Apparently, the old order of individual independence was at an end, to be replaced by the progressive preference for mutual interdependence. And since market forces were a cause of the Great Depression, by Roosevelt's reckoning, they should be replaced by national planning. Modern American conservatism, in response, should be rising to the defense of individual liberty and the role of markets.

Roosevelt was quick to point out that the Constitution should be no barrier to the revolutionary changes he had in mind. "Our Constitution is so simple and practical that it is possible always to meet extraordinary needs by changes in emphasis and arrangement without loss of essential form," Roosevelt continued in his first inaugural. Put differently, the time for constitutional reinterpretation had arrived. And the time for conservatives to defend the Constitution and the Bill of Rights of the Founding generation had also arrived, because the roots of the American order were at stake.

According to Roosevelt, the Framers bequeathed to us the constitutional doctrine that the end justifies the means and that all means are constitutional that are directed to a national emergency. And if it turns out that a rather broad interpretation of congressional powers is inadequate to solve the problem, Roosevelt would seek war powers: "I shall ask the Congress for the one remaining instrument to meet the crisis: broad executive power to wage a war against the emergency, as great as the power that would be given to me if we were in fact invaded by a foreign foe." At least Roosevelt lived in an era when it was still recognized that executive war powers required congressional approval.

HOOVER'S CONSTITUTION DAY ADDRESS

Former President Hoover, on September 17, 1935, gave a speech on Constitution Day in San Diego—as far as we know, the first time that a sitting or former president gave an address on Constitution Day. Two years later, FDR spoke on the sesquicentennial of the Constitution in 1937. And, as we shall see, an important concept used originally in Hoover's address reappeared in Roosevelt's message: the Constitution is a layman's document, not a lawyer's document. This "conversation" between Hoover and Roosevelt over constitutional interpretation, and who is to interpret the Constitution, is vital. This exchange captures an important part of the great divide that would take place between modern American liberalism and modern American conservatism after World War II. And at this initial stage of the conversation, Hoover sought to conserve the Constitution of both Washington and Lincoln from the Constitution according to the Roosevelt progressives.

Hoover's message on the 148th anniversary of the signing of the Constitution issued a warning rather than a commemoration of the signing. "The Constitution is under more vivid discussion than at any time since the years before the Civil War," he said. Hoover focused on what he called the attrition of the Bill of Rights after two years of the Roosevelt administration, arguing that there was a fundamental parallel with the Civil War era. For Hoover, the fate of the nation seventy-five years after the Civil War turned on the rights of man; in the 1930s, it concerned "the rights of the individual in relation to the government." Hoover found that "new philosophies and new theories of government have arisen in the world which militantly deny the validity of our principles." And these new approaches force Americans to revisit their principles, which were changing from the idea that rights in America were inherent to the view that rights are derived from the government itself. Hoover's response was straightforward: embedded in the Constitution itself are "the vital principles of the American System of liberty," and that "system is based upon certain unalienable freedoms and protections" that are beyond the reach of government.

These freedoms in the Bill of Rights that are beyond the reach of government are so obviously and unambiguously stated, he said, that "it does not require a lawyer to interpret those provisions. They are clear as the Ten Commandments." From Hoover's point of view, the language of the Constitution and the contemporaneous documentary evidence are such that a reasonable citizen would agree with Hoover that a lawyer is not necessary to interpret the language of the Declaration, the Constitution, or the Ten Amendments because the language is abundantly clear. Furthermore, these rights were already established by centuries of struggle; when "our forefathers . . . wrote the Declaration of Independence they boldly extended these rights." Later, they were "incorporated in black and white within the Constitution—and so became the Bill of Rights."

The following appeared in the *New York Times* newspaper version of the speech, but was, unfortunately, excluded from the book publication. It deserves reproduction at length:

Liberty never dies from direct attack. No one will dare rise tomorrow and say he is opposed to the Bill of Rights. Liberty dies from the encroachment and disregard of its safeguards. Its destruction can be no less potent from ignorance or desire to find shortcuts to jump over some immediate pressure.

In our country, abdication of its responsibilities and powers by Congress to the Executive, the repudiation by the government of its obligations, the centralization of authority into the Federal Government at the expense of local government, the building up of huge bureaucracies, the coercion or intimidation of citizens, are the same sort of first sapping of safeguards of human rights that have taken place in other lands. Here is the cause of anxiety and concern to the thinking citizens of the United States.

George Washington in his Farewell Address warned: "One method of assault may be to effect, in the form of the Constitution alterations which may impair the energy of the system and thus undermine that which cannot be directly overthrown."[1]

Hoover's Constitution Day address, then, was an invitation to the members of his audience to use their imaginations and locate the New Deal within the new philosophies of Europe that were antagonistic to the Bill of Rights and thus the Constitution. To be sure, "the functions of government must be readjusted from time to time to restrain the strong and protect the weak. That is the preservation of liberty itself." So some increases and adjustments in the functions of the federal government are to be expected over time. And, similarly, provisions of the Bill of Rights may well "jostle each other in course of changing national life—but their respective domains can be defined by virtue, by reason, and by law. And the freedom of men is not possible without virtue, reason, and law."

1. Associated Press, "Hoover's Warning of the Perils to Liberty," *New York Times,* September 18, 1935.

The message is pretty clear: the solution to the economic difficulties of the 1930s—consult the Constitution—does not lie in the expansion of the role of the federal government and the reduction of the realm of individual liberty. Rather, "the purification of Liberty from abuses, the restoration of the confidence in the rights of men, from which come the release of the dynamic forces of initiative and enterprise, are alone the methods through which these solutions can be found and the purpose of American life assured."

The provocative phrase, "the respective domains can be defined by virtue, by reason, and by law," and the statement that human freedom itself depends on the presence of "virtue, reason, and law," beg for explanation, but none is forthcoming. An explanation seems appropriate because, at the start of the speech, Hoover made the parallel between the Ten Amendments and the Ten Commandments and he certainly gave the impression that the meaning of each was self-evident. If we were but to read each innocently, as it were, the meaning would be simple and clear. Most importantly, the Constitution and the Bill of Rights are not a lawyer's document. They are a layman's document. That helps explain why states' rights and the Supreme Court are peripheral in Hoover's address, and the virtue of the people is important. But he leaves us wondering whether the layman needs to keep his virtual innocence or acquire an education in "virtue, reason, and law," all of which are essential conservative values.

Seventeen months later, Hoover delivered a speech in Chicago on February 20, 1937, called "Hands Off the Supreme Court." Surprisingly, given the context of the last fifty years, he did not say that the New Deal was unconstitutional because the Supreme Court said the New Deal was unconstitutional and therefore we had to have a hands-off approach to the issue. Rather, he saw a crisis of constitutional proportions in the same way that Abraham Lincoln—his hero—would see a constitutional crisis. Lincoln opposed the Dred Scott decision and he offered a constitutional amendment to overturn that decision rather than to simply accept what Judge Taney ordered or to have an executive order have the final say.

So Hoover framed the issue this way in 1937: shall we abide by the Constitution according to the interpretive skills of lawyers or the Constitution according to an honest reading by the layman? Shall "the President by the appointment of additional judges upon the Supreme Court . . . revise the Constitution—or whether change in the Constitution shall be submitted to the people as the Constitution itself provides"? Hoover thought that the revision of the Constitution should be decided by a constitutional amendment approved by the people or the state legislators rather than by a decision of an increased number of Roosevelt-favored judges. Hoover reminded his audience that the issue of stacking the Court "is not a lawyers' dispute over legalisms. This is the people's problem. And it is the duty of every citizen to concern himself with this question. It reaches the very center of his liberties." Senate Democrats agreed with Hoover that Roosevelt's attempt to stack the Supreme Court and get his three horses of the federal government operating smoothly in the same direction violated what Alexander Hamilton in "Federalist 78" referred to as "the manifest tenor" of the doctrine of separation of powers.

ROOSEVELT'S CONSTITUTION DAY ADDRESS

A month before Hoover's Chicago speech, Roosevelt reminded the audience in his second inaugural address that the whole point of the last four years was that "we dedicated ourselves . . . to a vision . . . to end by action, tireless and unafraid, the stagnation and despair of that day." And "we of the Republic" also recognized "a deeper need: the need to find through government the instrument of our united purpose to solve . . . the ever-rising problems of a complex civilization. Repeated attempts at their solution without the aid of government had left us baffled and bewildered." But the important question, as far as Hoover was concerned, was this one: was this fundamental alteration in the role of the federal government constitutional? By "constitutional," he meant more than merely, "What did the Supreme Court decide?"

Roosevelt's answer is clear: "The Constitution of 1787 did not make our democracy impotent." True enough, but the outcome of the Founding conversation was that the Constitution of 1787 did make our democracy constitutional. There are five auxiliary precautions that restrain an intemperate electoral majority from imposing its direct will on the whole population: legislative checks and balances, separation of political powers, an independent judiciary, federalism, and the Bill of Rights. But for Roosevelt, these auxiliary precautions are annoying impediments in the way of securing the general welfare. We ought not to fuss over mere means when the end objective is the implementation of "the new order of things" that was started on March 4, 1933. And what is at the core of this new order of things? It amounts to changing the moral climate of America from a pursuit of heedless self-interest to the establishment of a morally better world. And what does this better world look like? Roosevelt contrasted the current world where "I see one-third of a nation ill-housed, ill-clad, ill-nourished" to one where everyone is taken care of.

The scope of Roosevelt's constitutional revisionism is captured well in his speech on the 150th anniversary of the signing of the Constitution. In it, he recognized that the Framers created a constitutional democracy. But the survival of constitutional democracy requires the acceptance of three premises: 1) "the facts" show that government planning produces a higher standard of living than reliance on the market; so that 2) the real question is whether this ideal shall be secured by dictatorial government or democratic government; and 3) that constitutional democracy "must meet the insistence of the great mass of the people" concerning economic security. But can and will these premises be met under the Constitution? "Yes," says Roosevelt, emphatically.

At the center of Roosevelt's optimism is his claim that the Constitution "was a layman's document, not a lawyer's contract. That cannot be stressed too often." Accordingly, when it comes to "the fundamental powers of the new government," the Framers "used generality, implication, and statement of mere objectives, as intentional phrases which flexible statesmanship of the future, within the Constitution, could adapt to time and circumstance." This is the "living generation's expectation of government" concept of what today we would call "the living Constitution." Only back then, in 1937, it was the executive branch, armed with a mandate from the electorate, and guided by "flexible statesmanship," that was empowered to bring life to the Constitution and adapt it to the circumstances of the day, rather than the Supreme Court breathing life into the lifeless words of the Constitution.

So what is it that makes the original Constitution a layman's document rather than a lawyer's document? And why is a layman's interpretation preferable? "For one hundred and fifty years," Roosevelt said in his speech, "we have had an unending struggle between those who would preserve this original broad concept of the Constitution as a layman's instrument of government and those who would shrivel the Constitution into a lawyer's contract." Apparently, what makes the Constitution a layman's document is the absence of specific legal language trying, unsuccessfully, to stop the federal government from ultimately getting its way. Anyway, what is the point about preserving legal niceties when, in effect, Rome is burning? "The crisis of 1933 should make us understand that." Remember, the world belongs to the living and thus the Constitution belongs to us, we the people.

Both Hoover and Roosevelt agreed that the Constitution is a layman's document rather than a lawyer's document. What Roosevelt missed and Hoover understood is that the Constitution, in the final analysis, belongs to the two-thirds of the House plus two-thirds of the Senate plus three-fourths of the state legislatures required to amend the Constitution (or to three-fourths of specially called state ratifying conventions). Hoover's critique of Roosevelt is that the Constitution is a restraining document rather than a document that authorizes the majority at a presidential election to mandate the implementation of a progressive agenda.

The New Deal period is full of constitutional interpretations but virtually empty of constitutional amendments. By contrast, the Founding era, the Civil War era, and the early Progressive era each left behind a bundle of amendments that remind us of the place of these eras in the continuing American constitutional narrative. We are thinking about the first ten amendments for the Founding era; the thirteenth, fourteenth, and fifteenth amendments for the Civil War era; and the sixteenth through the nineteenth amendments for the early Progressive era. In the New Deal era, by contrast, the congressional powers of the Constitution in Article I, Section 8, and the executive powers of Article II, Section 2, were expanded by a reinterpretation of the Constitution rather than by constitutional amendment. This early reliance on constitutional interpretation rather than constitutional amendment set the tone for the creation and expansion of the administrative state.

PRESIDENT OBAMA AND THE SUPREME COURT

President Barack Obama called out the Supreme Court in his January 27, 2010, State of the Union address for its decision in the *Citizens United* case that "reversed a century of law to open the floodgates for special interests." With six justices in the room and Justice Samuel Alito mouthing "not true," it was a vivid reminder that battles over the Constitution and the courts are not relics of the New Deal era. In fact, the many high-profile matters that have been on the

Supreme Court's docket recently—health care, immigration, same-sex marriage—are not really so much about the issues themselves. Rather, they raise the underlying questions debated by Hoover and Roosevelt about how to interpret and apply the Constitution and the role of courts in doing so.

President Obama and the Democrats seemed to take a page right out of the Roosevelt playbook in defending the constitutionality of the Patient Protection and Affordable Care Act. The essence of their argument was that, since health care is a major national problem, Congress ought to be able to fix it, even though the Constitution does not grant the federal government power over health and welfare. Let's not let the Constitution get in the way when 45 million of "we the people" are "ill-healthed" or ill-insured! To the extent specific constitutional authority was needed, they pointed to the Commerce Clause or, alternatively, the taxing power to defend Congress's authority to enact a sweeping reform (and virtual federalization) of health care.

The Commerce Clause—from Article I, Section 8, of the Constitution, permitting Congress "to regulate commerce . . . among the several states"—was dormant for about 150 years before being roused by Roosevelt's expansive New Deal agenda. With the switch of one Supreme Court vote, a series of economic and other regulations that had previously been held unconstitutional was permitted under the Commerce Clause. Now the Commerce Clause no longer meant actual commerce but "activities . . . which so affect interstate commerce . . . as to make regulation appropriate" (*US v. Wrightwood Dairy Co., 1942*). Reaching its New Deal zenith, the court held that Congress could even regulate wheat grown on one's own land for family consumption (*Wickard v. Filburn, 1942*). As the minority opinion in the health care case by Justices Ruth Bader Ginsburg, Sonia Sotomayor, Stephen Breyer, and Elena Kagan concluded concerning this plenary power: "Since 1937, our precedent has recognized Congress's large authority to set the Nation's course in the economic and social welfare realm" (*National Federation of Independent Business v. Sebelius, 2012*).

The health care law pressed the New Deal understanding of the Commerce Clause even further, allowing Congress to regulate, in effect, no commerce—individual decisions not to purchase health insurance. Here, Chief Justice John G. Roberts, writing for the majority in the health care case, drew the line: "Construing the Commerce Clause to permit Congress to regulate individuals precisely because they are doing nothing would open a new and potentially vast domain to congressional authority." Of course this limit, which to Roberts and his four conservative colleagues seemed like the obvious intent of the Framers and the Constitution itself, came only one vote from being run over by the Court. And Roberts himself succumbed to judicial activism by, in effect, rewriting certain provisions of the health care law in order to save it constitutionally under Congress's taxing authority. The constitutional implications of that activism and expansion will not be fully understood for many years.

Other hot-button issues before the Supreme Court, such as immigration reform in Arizona (and elsewhere) and same-sex marriage, raise more directly questions of states' rights in a federalist system. While the New Deal greatly expanded federal power and regulation over economic matters, cases about same-sex marriage, medicinal marijuana, and the like ask who is in charge of social questions: the federal government or the states? Who should define marriage, and must that be uniform across the states? If Colorado wants to permit the use of marijuana and neighboring Kansas does not, must there be uniformity and, if so, under what constitutional power would Congress enforce this? In the case of immigration laws, where states such as Arizona are frustrated by the lack of enforcement from the federal government and want to join in the battle, does the federal supremacy clause prevent such collaboration? These continuing battles have been part of the federal-state tug of war from the beginning, though states have lost far more than they have won.

IS THE CONSTITUTION AN EMPOWERING DOCUMENT OR A RESTRAINING DOCUMENT?

At the same time these fundamental constitutional questions are being wrestled with in the courts, there is a growing narrative in the academic and political worlds that further threatens traditional notions of constitutional governance. The modern debate was energized by Franklin Roosevelt's notion that the most important words in the Constitution are "we the people" and that the people should be free to change constitutional governance more or less at will. And the people should not be confined to the cumbersome process of amending the Constitution—which requires a two-thirds vote of each house of Congress and a three-fourths vote of the states—in order to bend constitutional governance to their will.

For example, the National Popular Vote bill is being advanced in state legislatures as an obvious end-run around the Electoral College. This bill, when enacted in enough states to tally the 270 electoral votes needed to elect a president, would require each signatory state to cast its electoral votes in favor of the winner of the national popular vote. This would, in effect, eliminate the electoral vote mandated by the Constitution and would elect the winner of the national popular vote as president, all without following the constitutional process of amending the Constitution. As of this writing, nine states representing 132 electoral votes (or nearly half the votes needed) have enacted the bill.

This misguided campaign is wrong in both its objectives and its methods. The Founders intentionally established a republic, not a pure democracy; they incorporated several checks and balances, and carefully balanced governmental powers, so that the "cool and deliberate sense of the community" would prevail ("Federalist 63"). In Congress, for example, they established the people's House of Representatives, based upon population counts, but also the Senate with its membership divided evenly among the states. Similarly, in the election for president, the Constitution provides for a popular vote for the people, but an electoral vote by state. So electoral voting—there is actually no reference to an "Electoral College" in the Constitution—is a vital ingredient of the federalist system.

Further, the electoral system produces benefits in the way campaigns and elections operate. In the final weeks of a presidential campaign, where do the candidates go? They travel to battleground states large and small all over the country, arguing immigration in New Mexico, industrial development in Michigan, retirement benefits in Florida, and the like. In a national popular vote, how would the final weeks of the campaign be conducted? By television and Internet, primarily, with visits to a handful of large population centers such as New York and Los Angeles. And the problem of recounts would be greatly magnified in a national popular vote, with the specter of a weeks-long Florida recount in 2000 multiplied many times over in time and complexity in what would inevitably become a national recount.

The case for the "clever" National Popular Vote bill, as described by the *Los Angeles Times* shortly after the 2012 election, is that America has grown up now and can shed the unnecessary federalism protections designed by the Founders in the Constitution. The Electoral College system is not sufficiently democratic and "offends modern sensibilities," the *Times* editorialized.[2] It is anachronistic, an unpleasant relic of a past that included slavery and denial of the vote to women, as though this were the real case for one of the several checks and balances the Founders, suspicious of pure

---

2. *Los Angeles Times,* "President, By Popular Vote," November 12, 2012, http://articles.latimes.com/2012/nov/12/opinion/la-ed-popular-vote-20121112.

democracy, included in the Constitution. In order to modernize the Constitution, then, proponents of the National Popular Vote bill would pass over the Constitution's own mechanism for change, the amendment, because that is too difficult to accomplish, they say. And, to carry out their "clever" end-run around the Constitution, they would use an interstate compact, arguably in violation of yet another provision of the Constitution, which allows the use of such compacts only with the consent of Congress (not contemplated by the proponents).

On this matter of electoral voting, by the way, there is a perfectly constitutional alternative: states could decide to split up their electoral votes rather than award them winner-takes-all. Under the Constitution, there is no national election for president, but rather fifty-one (including the District of Columbia) state elections. Each state is empowered under the Constitution to decide how it will allocate its electoral votes. All but two, Maine and Nebraska, allocate all their electoral votes to the winner of their popular vote, but this is not required. Maine and Nebraska allocate one electoral vote for the winner of each congressional district, and two for the winner of the state popular vote. If you've ever seen a map of the United States by counties, you've noticed that we aren't really divided red versus blue, but there is a lot of purple. So this kind of allocation of electoral votes would seem to reflect more accurately the division of votes on the ground, as opposed to the more artificial decision to give all a state's electoral votes to one candidate. It would also make some states more competitive in presidential campaigns. When this was raised by Republicans following the 2012 campaign, it was dismissed as some kind of political maneuver. But in fact it is a perfectly legal and constitutional change, and arguably an improvement in both the campaign and the electoral process.

The National Popular Vote bill is but one example of a kind of "democratic" overhaul many would like to undertake on our constitutional system. Recent books by three leading academics illustrate the underlying philosophical basis and even offer a game plan for dramatic change: Sanford Levinson's *Our Undemocratic Constitution*, Larry Sabato's *A More Perfect Constitution*, and Louis Michael Seidman's *On Constitutional Disobedience*. Levinson's use of the word "undemocratic" in the title, augmented by the subtitle, "Where the Constitution Goes Wrong (And How We the People Can Correct It)," tells most of what we need to know to understand his book and this movement. Essentially Levinson argues that structural impediments to democracy need to be eliminated: the US Senate (small states with few people get the same say as large states), the presidential veto (one person's view stops the will of the majority), the Electoral College (the winner of the popular vote may lose the election), and the difficulty of enacting constitutional amendments.

Political analyst Larry Sabato goes even further in his book, *A More Perfect Constitution*, arguing that the Constitution needs an extreme makeover and offering twenty-three specific revisions to that end. First, he wants to boost the Senate from 100 members to 135, and more than double the membership of the House of Representatives to an even 1,000. There are also term limits for Congress, a new election cycle, and, while we're at it, only one six-year term for the president, with the possibility of a two-year performance bonus. But he's just getting started: a line-item veto, a balanced budget amendment, a mandatory two-year national service program, and more. In sum, he wants to make the Constitution fairer (read "more democratic") and more effective. He would accomplish all this by calling a constitutional convention—the Constitution's own amendment process is too difficult and ineffective for him—and putting these ideas on the table.

Professor Louis Michael Seidman blames the government's inability to manage the "fiscal cliff" that confronted the government early in 2013 on the "archaic, idiosyncratic and downright evil provisions" of our Constitution. He suggests today's leaders follow some of their predecessors, like Franklin D. Roosevelt, who extended "federal power beyond anything the Framers imagined" and who "threaten[ed] the Supreme Court when it stood in the way of his New Deal legislation."[3] Unlike most Americans, according to the polls, this constitutional law professor would place his trust instead in Congress, the president, and the Supreme Court.

This philosophical battle is essentially fought over whether America should remain a federal republic—with the careful balances and separations of power incorporated by the Founders— or be turned into more of a pure national democracy. It is easy to argue that individual elements of the republic are not democratic— small states having as many US senators as large ones, an electoral vote that may not be consonant with the national popular vote—but, taken together, they form a federal democratic republic that has endured and prospered for 225 years. It's not that the Constitution is antiquated and in need of updating; it's that some feel a federal republic makes it too difficult for the people to make sweeping structural changes—which is, of course, precisely what the Founders intended. This brings us back to the Roosevelt view, that "we the people" own the Constitution and ought to be able to do with it as we will. But the Founders' view, which conservatives should embrace, is that the Constitution is a founding, defining document which provides its own mechanism for change: the amendment process. Roosevelt sought to redefine the notion of a constitutional republic by reinterpretation rather than amendment, and that is the goal of many progressives and academics today.

Benjamin Franklin reportedly responded, when asked what kind of government the Founders had established: "A republic if you can keep it." And, indeed, keeping the republic is one of the major constitutional challenges of our day. Have you noticed that there really

3. Louis Michael Seidman, "Let's Give Up on the Constitution," *New York Times*, December 30, 2012, A19.

is no constituency for good government or constitutional processes? There are constituencies for every conceivable position on substantive issues such as gun control or same-sex marriage. And people seem perfectly willing to undertake most any measure needed to press their position. For example, a few years ago, Congress passed, and the president signed, a bill to open the federal courts to one specific person: Terri Schiavo and the battle over her life support. They did this even though the matter had been heard before many courts and the law did not permit federal jurisdiction for this. What we need in these matters is more "constitutional" conservatives, more people who will stand up for federalism and proper constitutional processes, rather than people who simply want to press their particular issues in order to win at all costs.

THE CONSTITUTIONAL PENDULUM SWINGS SLOWLY AND UNEVENLY

The Supreme Court's ultimate support for the New Deal's expansion of federal authority essentially continued unchecked for fifty years, even accelerating during the Warren Court years with not only *Brown v. Board of Education* but also with key decisions about contraception, rights of the accused, obscenity, and so forth. That is to say, after a long period before the New Deal when the Commerce Clause and other sources of federal power lay dormant, there was another long period in which essentially no Supreme Court opinions imposed significant limitations on the federal government. Then, as constitutional scholar Erwin Chemerinsky has pointed out, for a decade from 1992–2002 the Rehnquist Court limited federal power under the Commerce Clause, revived the Tenth Amendment on states' rights, and expanded state sovereign immunity.[4] Then

---

4. Erwin Chemerinsky, "Keynote Address," 41 *Willamette Law Review*, 2005, 827–828.

little happened for another ten years until the health care reform decision again limited federal power under the Commerce Clause, while upholding it under the taxing power.

While the court's decisions themselves have been one battle-ground of constitutional law, the justices have also sharpened the debate by discussing more explicitly their philosophy of constitutional interpretation. Justice Antonin Scalia has changed the terms of the debate by his practice of originalism: what did the Constitution mean at the time it was adopted? That this question is even asked, much less followed in many Supreme Court decisions, is a significant turn in jurisprudence. Liberal justices counter with their view, very much a Roosevelt "we the people" interpretation, that ours is a living Constitution subject to change with new circumstances. Of course the balance between these two depends very much on who is president, holding the power of Supreme Court appointments, again a matter Roosevelt attempted to influence with his court-packing plan and open advocacy of results he wanted from the court. If not the former, Obama has controversially attempted the latter, criticizing the court's decision in the *Citizens United* case and opining on the health care decision before the judicial process was complete.

But it's important to note that the pendulum of judicial review of federal power does not swing back and forth evenly. It is more like three or four steps toward greater federal power, than one step back toward limitations. This is true in part because Republican presidents have made appointments—David Souter, Anthony Kennedy, Sandra Day O'Connor—whose constitutional views either were not as conservative as expected or whose opinions drifted toward greater federal power over time. Another factor is that one element of a conservative judicial philosophy is to honor precedents, even when those precedents are liberal. As Judge Richard Posner of the United States Court of Appeals for the Seventh Circuit has observed, liberal judges ratchet up constitutional rights and federal power, and they are followed by periods of restraint that, in effect, solidify what went before, making it difficult to undo liberal expansion. More recent conservative appointments—Clarence Thomas, Antonin Scalia, Samuel Alito—seemed less constrained by what they viewed as inappropriate precedents, making the court a more dynamic playing field.

Conclusion

In "Federalist 78," Alexander Hamilton opined that the judiciary, not having the power of the purse or sword, would be the "least dangerous" of the branches. Moreover, it would be tied down by precedent and the reality that Congress controls the appellate jurisdiction of the court. The anti-federalist Brutus argued that the court has the potential to become the most dangerous branch. What if the members of the court decide that it is the ultimate interpreter of what the Constitution means? We get a reversal of "real" power in the constitutional pyramid. Today it often seems like the pyramid has indeed reversed and that most of the key decisions of the day await resolution by the Supreme Court. The courts have moved from their historic role as brakes on unconstitutional action by the Congress to engines of social change, be it drawing up maps of school desegregation or announcing newly discovered rights of privacy/abortion or same-sex marriage. It is little wonder, then, that the courts have become arguably the central battleground today on conservative versus liberal philosophies of government, especially pertaining to social issues and government power.

Today's constitutional struggle is clearly a child of the New Deal era. As Harvard political scientist Harvey Mansfield aptly put it: "The American Founders wanted people to live under the Constitution, but the progressives want the Constitution to live under the American people."[5] When faced with a difficult question, especially

5. Ahmari, "The Crisis of American Self-Government."

regarding a social issue, progressives now prefer to go to the courts rather than the legislature. Why? Because legislation might vary from state to state, and bills can always be amended. But if a federal court declares that something is a right under the federal Constitution, it becomes established constitutional law and is nearly impossible to change or revoke. Even many progressives now acknowledge, for example, that establishing a woman's right to an abortion under strained interpretations of constitutional law, rather than allowing legislatures to debate and decide over time, has led to decades of battles and strife over the issue. But now, in the case of gay marriage, even with states beginning to act politically in its favor, there is the press to have this declared by courts to be a matter of constitutional rights. Again, there is no restraint, no moderation, no respect for constitutional processes, only a desire to win on the issue at hand.

CHAPTER 5

The 2012 Election and the Future of Conservatism

Following the 2012 reelection of Barack Obama, many proclaimed the death of modern American conservatism. The *Titanic* is sinking, said one commentator; the conservative arguments put forth in the campaign will soon be relics in a museum, wrote another. Demography is destiny, many said, and conservatism is the realm of old white men whose day is gone. This is the day of the young, of immigrants, of people of color, of women, who vote progressive, not conservative. A standard refrain was that conservatism needs to change both its methods and its message if it ever hopes to be successful again. In short, many called for an extreme makeover for modern American conservatism.

Others see in history a swinging pendulum, understanding that what is not in favor today may well rule the day tomorrow. In particular, election results often swing wildly from side to side, with one party racking up major victories in a presidential election, only to lose ground to the other side in the midterm elections a mere two years later. This is just what happened with Obama's win in 2008, followed by the formation of the Tea Party and record losses for Democrats in 2010. As former British Prime Minister Harold Wilson put it, "A week in politics is a long time."

As the two coauthors of this book, long-time colleagues and friends, we confess that each of us had a different take on the consequences of the 2012 election and the future prospects for conservatism. One of us believes that a new majority of more liberal voters—younger people, ethnic minorities, wealthy elites, those receiving significant income from the government—are on the ascendancy. For him, this is a *No Country for Old Men* moment. He feels like the sheriff in that movie (or book) who now sees extreme irresponsibility among voters and in government. He despairs of his ability to make any real difference about it. He feels it's time to leave California, in his view the exemplar of irresponsible governance, and retire to the most livable red state he can find.

Our other coauthor sees no reason to turn away from his *Mr. Smith Goes to Washington* life and career. In his case, he went to the academy in California, rather than to government in Washington, D.C., but he retains his optimism about making a difference in the lives of graduate students and high school teachers, teaching the beauty of the American Founding and its constitutional republic. He sees no need for an extreme makeover of modern American conservatism, nor to leave his beautiful California beach community for life in some cold, rugged red state. The American people are center-right, he says, and though they may get carried away in this or that election, given the right candidates and moment, they will return to their more conservative roots.

CONSERVATISM: OF POLITICS, POLICY, AND PRINCIPLE

For starters, we need to understand that conservatism operates at different levels in varied ways. In a sense, politics is only the shallow topsoil of the public arena. Polling demonstrates that voters are blown about by conventional wisdom, the latest speech or poll, or even a candidate's hairstyle. Elections do, as they say, have consequences, and the short-term future (two to four years) may be decided there, but generally nothing long-lasting is decided in a single election. In addition, we must understand that a political philosophy, such as conservatism, doesn't really stand for election. Individual candidates run for office, and political parties do battle in elections. But ideas and philosophies are, or at least should be, much deeper than that. Republicans are not consistently conservative—in fact, as noted in chapter 3, large growth in government has often occurred under Republican presidents. And Democrats are not always liberal. So it would seem naïve, at best, to assume that the long-term fate of a political philosophy such as modern American conservatism would be settled on a single election day in November 2012.

As a consequence, conservatism is not likely to be resurrected, or even significantly strengthened, by tinkering at the political level. When people say Mitt Romney was not a great candidate, or did not run a strong campaign, that may have little to do with conservatism, per se. For one thing, there is a view strongly held by many that Romney himself was not truly a conservative candidate. Both his record as governor of Massachusetts and his evolving stands on a number of issues made him seem more like a pragmatic businessman than a political conservative. Further, the fact that Obama won the election does not mean that this was a highly ideological campaign in which political philosophies were the decisive factor. Some argue that the 2012 election was very close until Romney's private remarks to donors about 47 percent of Americans being dependent became public and Obama looked presidential in his response to Hurricane Sandy. The point is that campaigns and elections should not be ignored, but they more often turn on the state of the economy, or incumbency, or the attractiveness of the candidate, or the effectiveness of the campaign, and are not necessarily good barometers of how a particular political ideology sits with the American public. Still, as candidates and parties try to solve their political problems, it is important to see whether conservative principles are helped or hurt in the process.

At a deeper level is the realm of policy, where particular approaches to issues and problems are developed and where ideologies such as conservatism are very much in play. Unfortunately, the political landscape at the moment seems to be choking out thoughtful policy development, not only from a conservative point of view but more broadly. The Democrats don't really have a coherent set of policies now, other than to raise taxes on the rich and try to "stimulate" (a politically correct word for "spend") our way toward economic recovery. But they do appear to be more in touch with voters' concerns, even if they do not have policy solutions for them.

The Republicans essentially do not want to raise taxes on anyone at any time, and say they want to tame government spending, though a lot of the increased spending happened on their watch in the first place. Romney started his fall presidential campaign with a fifty-nine-point plan for the economy, which sounds more like what a consultant would deliver to a paying client than what a candidate should offer as a coherent set of policies. Finally he got it down to five points. Republican vice presidential candidate Paul Ryan was the closest candidate we've had to a policy wonk since Bill Clinton, having published a detailed plan on the budget and economy. But conservatives could very much use a candidate, or a set of leaders, who could advance clear, coherent, conservative approaches to the policy issues of the day, including immigration, gun control, the budget, and so forth.

At the deepest level are the principles that animate a particular philosophy, such as conservatism. Here is where conservatives have a lot of work to do. One problem is that conservatism is, in many ways, more of a reactionary philosophy than a proactive one. As William F. Buckley famously said, "A conservative is someone who stands athwart history yelling, Stop." Since its primary purpose is to conserve liberty, and also the traditions and institutions that help protect individual liberty, the message of conservatism is often in reaction against government efforts that would harm liberty. So its principles come off as reactionary and negative—no taxes, turn back the clock on abortion, and so forth. Another challenge is that some conservatives, such as social conservatives, have a different set of principles than classic or fiscal conservatives. So finding a common set of principles for conservatives, one that seems to suit the times, is a challenge that has to be confronted with regularity. In order to work that out in these times, it seems important for conservatives to address a series of difficult questions.

DOES LIBERTY STILL RESONATE?

For Edmund Burke, the father of modern conservatism, the essence of conservatism was individual liberty. The Founders, in the words of the Declaration of Independence, sought "life, liberty, and the pursuit of happiness." Herbert Hoover, who was resisting the vast government expansion and intrusion of Roosevelt's New Deal, entitled his volume of writings *The Challenge to Liberty*. So for 150 years, from the Founding to the New Deal, liberty resonated in America. Why do immigrants still want to come to the United States today? For the opportunities that liberty provides.

But does individual liberty still resonate today as a principle worth fighting and voting for? Do younger people, who have grown up knowing only big government, appreciate a philosophy that sees government as a potential threat to liberty? Has individual liberty become merely an abstraction that no longer speaks powerfully to the American people? There are three basic liberties we have historically held dear: economic, religious, and political. But do people really see the threats to them today?

It is no longer enough to merely repeat the conservative principles. It has become necessary to animate, illustrate, and remake the case. When a decorator said I could only use certain kinds of handles in my shower, by law, that helped illustrate that I live in a much more highly regulated state than I would like. In New York City, Mayor Bloomberg wants to regulate the size of soft drinks. When your monthly paycheck dropped dramatically in January of 2013, that was a vivid reminder that taxes were going up. When you work well into April, and in some states even into early May, simply to pay your taxes, that's a powerful reminder of how much government you have, and how much you are paying for it. This is a threat to economic freedom, to the fruits of one's labor, but that message is not getting through.

Young people, in particular, do not readily see the twin problems of too much government and too little individual freedom. A Pew Research Center survey reported in November 2012 that voters under age thirty are the only age group in which a majority said government should do more to fix problems. Of course, young voters will soon enough be older voters, and will experience higher taxes and more restrictions. But this is a reminder that the case for limited government and for individual freedom must be remade in every generation. These young voters need to see the attraction of churches and nonprofits and other intermediary civic associations that conservatives love more dearly than just deferring problems to the government. So even at the core of conservative principles—individual freedom—there is much work to be done to sharpen the focus and communicate the message in clearer and more compelling terms. Individual liberty, to many, has become merely an abstraction.

IS IT TIME TO GIVE UP ON TRADITION, VIRTUE, AND SOCIAL VALUES?

Younger voters are raising the question whether conservatism needs to give up on its effort to, as they see it, tell people how to live.

Of course the libertarian branch of conservatism has long embraced the notion that individual freedom should include the freedom to live as you want, without interference from government. Still other conservatives might not characterize themselves as libertarian, but would say they are fiscal conservatives but social moderates (or even liberals), again willing to abide a variety of individual decisions about lifestyle. Social and Christian conservatives have become an active and important voting bloc since the 1970s, attempting to define conservatism to include positions on abortion, gay marriage, stem cell research, and so forth. These positions, it is argued, especially turn off younger voters, who identify more with liberals (or, if they knew more about them, libertarians) on these social issues. Herbert Hoover's great-granddaughter, Margaret Hoover, published a book in 2011 making this case: *American Individualism: How a New Generation of Conservatives Can Save the Republican Party.*

But one of the dilemmas of conservatism is that it has long embraced both individual freedom and the traditions and values that uphold it. Edmund Burke embraced a "manly, moral, regulated liberty," understanding that tradition actually strengthened freedom. The Founders understood that, as Benjamin Franklin put it, "only a virtuous people are capable of freedom." So long before the emergence of social conservatives or the Christian right, there was an understanding that liberty, or doing as you wish, required the restraining influences of virtue and tradition, or doing as you ought or has long been done. Conservatives, then, need to be cautious about throwing out the baby of virtue and tradition with the bathwater of social and religious conservatism.

Peter Berkowitz, in his recent book *Constitutional Conservatism,* attempts to bring into one tent the two primary branches of conservatism: libertarianism and social conservatism. A key part of his approach is that he would require social conservatives to accept that the sexual revolution is here to stay and to quit fighting that battle on the political stage. But if your religious understanding is that God forbids abortion or contraception, it seems like a bridge too far to say you must give up a fight against having government, or your tax money, support and advance those practices.

It does seem important, however, for conservatives to find a way not to insist that government support certain specific religious or social beliefs, without giving up entirely on the broader virtues and traditions that support a free society. Perhaps the focus could be more on some of the public virtues such as honesty and moderation that truly allow a free society to function. Or, more practically, perhaps social conservatives need to be challenged to temper their views with traditional conservative notions of federalism, which calls on government to act only when individual action is insufficient, then insisting that the lower levels of government act when federal action is not truly needed. So, then, social conservatives might be discouraged from pressing their views at the federal level in favor of the Defense of Marriage Act, for example, recognizing that marriage should really be a matter of state policy. Social conservatives would then have to accept a variety of social policies in the states. Similarly, conservatives, who preach against judicial activism, should accept the self-discipline not to turn every question into a federal lawsuit. This is a kind of moderation that might allow conservatives to be faithful to their core principles, yet reach a broader public. As difficult as these steps may be, it seems far preferable for conservatives to attempt to work through the difficult dilemmas of values in a free society rather than throw tradition and virtue out of their politics altogether.

IS THE CONSTITUTION A GATHERING PLACE OR A STUMBLING BLOCK?

As noted in chapter 2, there is a view, especially in the academy, that the Constitution is an old, anachronistic document that is not relevant to the issues of our day. Some would go further and argue that, having been drafted by landowning men who would not abolish slavery, the Constitution was flawed from the beginning. Those are more extreme views, but even people in the middle wonder about seemingly abstract notions of federalism such as the Electoral College or limitations imposed on Congress by the tenth and fourteenth amendments. If we have a major national issue such as health care, why can't the federal government step in and act? Why would it be constrained by a 225-year-old document?

But the Constitution must be a central part of the conservative case going forward. It is primarily through the Constitution that we find balances of power, checks and balances, and limits on the power of government. These are the very tools that would enable conservatives to continue to wage the battle that is central for them: the campaign for limited government. In fact, it would behoove conservatives to be ever more active in civic education efforts, since constitutional principles have become another of those abstractions that many citizens fail to appreciate. Tellingly, when we coauthored a newspaper quiz for Constitution Day a few years ago, a friend called to say he had failed the test, but his girlfriend, an immigrant, had passed with flying colors. Why? Because she had taken the required dose of civic education needed for citizenship. The problem with the Constitution is not what it says; it's that people don't know what it says and fail to appreciate its meaning and value.

Another way in which the Constitution can be a way forward for conservatives is its value in uniting the disparate elements of the movement. There are fiscal conservatives, social conservatives, Christian conservatives, and libertarians, just to name a few branches of the conservative tree. But one trunk that could sustain all the branches would be strong allegiance to the Constitution. The First Amendment's free exercise of religion empowers Christian conservatives. The Tenth Amendment's reservation of power to states and the individual is the anthem of conservatives who want limited government. The taxing power, the interstate commerce test, balances of power, checks and balances, they're all there in the Constitution. Defending, explaining, and teaching the Constitution should be right near the top of the conservative agenda going forward.

IS THERE REASON FOR OPTIMISM ABOUT THE FUTURE OF CONSERVATISM?

We know there are reasons for despair about the future of conservatism in America. After Ronald Reagan, by acclamation the last great conservative president, passed the office to his vice president, George H. W. Bush, the more conservative candidate for president has lost four of six elections. Chief Justice Roberts's surprising decision affirming the constitutionality of health care reform, followed by Romney's loss in 2012, pretty well cements the addition of health care to the permanent and expensive roster of government entitlements, the most historic such development in nearly fifty years. The several branches of conservatism are difficult to hold together, and its appeal to a younger and more ethnically diverse electorate seems less than compelling.

Still, there are reasons for optimism about the future of American conservatism. In a symposium in its January 2013 edition, *Commentary* shared the perspectives of fifty-three leading American thinkers and writers on "What is the Future of Conservatism in the Wake of the 2012 Election?" Some thoughtful responses affirm both a reason for optimism as well as some concrete steps that might be taken toward a hopeful future for conservatism. For example, Larry Arnn, president of Hillsdale College, states that conservatism "must repudiate absolutely this system of limitless government. . . . It must proclaim without ceasing the good of freedom and the danger to it." We agree. And that was certainly Hoover's view in the

1930s, one that captures the enduring core of modern American conservatism.

Michael Barone, resident fellow at the American Enterprise Institute, points out that the economic difficulties may draw a line in the liberal sand that will allow conservatives to gain some traction. As he says, "The dire fiscal plight of the federal government and the unsustainable trajectory of entitlement programs give them more leverage than they would have from their House majority alone." AEI President Arthur C. Brooks lays out a challenge: conservatives must patiently and persistently change the conventional wisdom that holds that the free enterprise system is fundamentally unfair and that the entitlement state is morally acceptable and economically sustainable. This is an important reminder that conservatives have a lot of work to do, not on the surface level of politics so much as in the deeper trenches of values.

One set of views holds that the present road of progressivism will ultimately reach a dead end, offering conservatives an opportunity to step forward with an alternative course. As James Piereson, head of the Simon Foundation, says, conservatives are well prepared to "step into the breach when liberals run the system aground," as Reagan and former British Prime Minister Margaret Thatcher did. "The day is fast approaching," Piereson continues, when conservatives will be called upon to play that role again. "The postwar order is unraveling, America's economic engine has stalled, but the baby boomers are retiring, and the world still needs US leadership." Political scientist James Ceaser, at the University of Virginia, told a conference in December 2012 that there will be a day of reckoning—a result of taxes, a slow economy, fear of losing benefits, weakness or error in foreign policy—when conservatives will again need to step forward.

It appears that President Obama intends to press a more strident progressive agenda in his second term than he did in his first, which may open new opportunities for conservatives. As

President George W. Bush discovered when he used his reelection to seek major changes to Social Security, it is easy to overplay the mandate of a close election. And President Obama may well be on track to do just that. Obama's second inaugural address called for a kind of collectivism that he believes would make America a fairer and more democratic nation. He wants more taxes on the wealthy and an array of new programs that he said in his 2013 State of the Union message would not add a single dime to the federal budget, a claim that strains credulity. By this theory, progressivism will again self-destruct, and conservatives need only stay the course and await their moment.

In sum, we agree with Jennifer Rubin, who writes the "Right Turn" blog for the *Washington Post,* when she said, "If modern conservatism, in its essence, is the defense of freedom and security by limited government and the cultivation of a virtuous populace through intermediary institutions (family, church and synagogue, and civic organizations), then its currency is strong."

STILL RELEVANT AFTER ALL THESE YEARS

Conservatives would do well to ask themselves several historical questions. First, why, after 225 years, are the Founders still relevant? The answer would seem to be the power of first principles, the Founders' ideals of individual liberty and limited government, which should still be important to conservatives. But intriguingly, why, after eighty years, should the New Deal still be relevant? Is it because, in a time of crisis and fear, Franklin Roosevelt won several elections and took advantage of the opportunity to reinvent American domestic and constitutional policy? And that we still live under that same basic framework of his high-tax, high-regulation, high-welfare, high-entitlement state today?

What then is the relevance of conservatism today? Is it just to be ready when progressivism falters, as it did when Jimmy Carter gave way to Ronald Reagan? Is it merely to set up a loyal opposition, to limit the excesses of progressivism, to "stand athwart history yelling, Stop," as William F. Buckley suggested? In this sense, it is possible to see the appeal of progressivism, which has a more optimistic view of the nature of man and the possibility of steady, scientific progress. Conservatives, by contrast, understand that human beings need restraint, which often comes off as a more pessimistic face. Progressives are good at finding stories of individual suffering and turning those into campaigns for changes to public policy. If someone isn't doing well financially, it must be the fault of the system. Failure to achieve equality must be a market failure and so, progressives say, clearly we need more government regulation. We must do something! Conservatives would trust individuals and churches and civic associations to do something effective about these cases of individual suffering rather than developing government programs to address them.

We identify with the conservative Willmoore Kendall, a practical Oklahoman who believed Americans carried their tradition, their moral sense, indeed their conservatism, "in their hips."[1] Their vote may be captured by some charismatic progressive—a Roosevelt, an Obama—but at the end of the day, we are still a center-right people, in our hips. We may vote to tax the wealthy and give the rest of us an easier ride, but we also want forces to counteract that impulse, lest we get carried away and ruin the economy or, worse, the republic. We may want freedom, but we also want restraint, lest we run the ship of state aground. This, we argue, is the role of modern American conservatism. It speaks from our hips. It is the restraint, the brakes, the counterbalance when the intellectuals and politicians and progressives get carried away. Conservatism allows what the Founders called the cool and deliberate sense of the

---

1. Willmoore Kendall, *The Conservative Affirmation in America* (Chicago: Henry Regnery Company, 1963).

community to win out over time, rather than seeing the country carried away by the politics or factions of the moment.

In that sense, modern American conservatism is just what we've been saying needs to be preserved. It is the Constitution with its checks and balances, its balances of power, its restraints on government. It is our traditions and values and virtues that make it possible to live responsibly within a free republic. It is our instinct to limit government lest it run over us. It is the set of boundaries in which the game can be played.

And so conservatism is a voice, an influence, a set of ideas that must be healthy and vital in order for the republic to stay on track. Modern American conservatism started with Herbert Hoover, a prophetic voice in the progressive wilderness of the New Deal, calling Americans back from excessive government, the regulated life, the temptation toward the totalitarianisms of Europe offered by the New Deal. And it became a movement in the 1950s, led by Russell Kirk, Friedrich von Hayek, William F. Buckley, Milton Friedman, and others. It produced a presidential candidate, Barry Goldwater, in the midst of the progressive excesses of Lyndon Johnson's Great Society. It delivered its first president, Ronald Reagan, when Jimmy Carter could not command the ship of state effectively. It produced a "Contract with America" that limited the span of Bill Clinton's reach, even prompting him to say that the era of big government was over. Its voice was heard clearly on the Supreme Court through Chief Justice William Rehnquist, Antonin Scalia, and others. When Barack Obama won his first term, it spawned a Tea Party and won the midterm elections.

And now it prepares itself for the next chapter. If it is wise, it allows others to worry about electoral strategies and politics and it digs deeper into policy and principle. Perhaps, after eight years of progressive policies, the pendulum swings back toward conservatism. Or maybe the progressives overstep their mandate and things turn more quickly to conservatives. It could be that with several conservatives serving as governors, our states will once again become powerful laboratories and produce the policies that will lead to a resurgence of conservatism. Perhaps it will require a decade for conservatives to work at the deepest levels on conventional wisdom and turn things back toward limited government, balanced budgets, moral and traditional restraint, and, most of all, individual liberty. Ultimately it will require a candidate who embodies the principles of conservatism and can communicate them in compelling ways to the American electorate. This is both the legacy and the future of modern American conservatism.

ABOUT THE AUTHORS

GORDON LLOYD is a professor of public policy at the School of Public Policy at Pepperdine University. The coauthor of three books on the American Founding, and sole author of a book on the New Deal, he also has numerous articles, reviews, and opinion-editorials to his credit. His latest coauthored book, *The Two Narratives of Political Economy,* was published in 2010. Gordon is the creator of four websites on the origin and adoption of the Constitution and Bill of Rights. He also serves on the National Advisory Council for the Walter and Leonore Annenberg Presidential Learning Center through the Ronald Reagan Presidential Foundation.

DAVID DAVENPORT is counselor to the director and a research fellow at the Hoover Institution at Stanford University. He previously served as president of Pepperdine University, where he was also a professor of law and public policy. He is a regular columnist for Forbes.com, having previously been a columnist for the *San Francisco Chronicle* and Scripps Howard News Service. He is also a contributing editor to Townhall.com and delivers regular radio commentaries for the Salem Radio Network. He has contributed chapters to Hoover Press books and articles for *Policy Review* and is coauthor of the book *Shepherd Leadership.*

INDEX